VISUAL C++
in easy steps

Alan Kelly

COMPUTER
STEP

In easy steps is an imprint of Computer Step
Southfield Road . Southam
Warwickshire CV33 0FB . England

Tel: 01926 817999 Fax: 01926 817005
http://www.computerstep.com

Notice of Liability
Every effort has been made to ensure that this book contains accurate
and current information. However, Computer Step and the author shall
not be liable for any loss or damage suffered by readers as a result of
any information contained herein.

Trademarks
Microsoft® and Windows® are registered trademarks of Microsoft
Corporation. All other trademarks are acknowledged as belonging to
their respective companies.

Printed and bound in the United Kingdom

ISBN 1-874029-88-1

Contents

Getting Started

This chapter offers some useful information about which options to install with Visual C++ and shows you the basics of the user interface.

Chapter One

Covers

Installation Options

If you have already installed Visual C++ and you want to get your hands dirty you can skip straight to Chapter Two where you will start generating your first project.

There are two installation types that you can choose from with Visual C++:

Typical installation
This will install the most typically used components of Visual C++ which use between 235 and 262MB of hard disk space.

Custom
Allows you to choose which components of Visual C++ are installed onto your system. Installing every component will occupy approximately 375MB of disk space, so you may want to choose not to install certain components.

What can you leave out to save disk space?
There are some options that, if you decide not to install them, can cause problems later on when you come to develop applications. This means that you will end up having to go through the installation process again.

HANDY TIP

Unicode is specific to Windows NT and is not supported fully on Windows.

There are, however, many components which can be omitted without any adverse effects. For example, you do not *need* to install the Unicode libraries for the Microsoft Foundation Classes (MFCs) – this will automatically save you over 67MB of disk space!

If you want to save even more space, you could make a decision before you start developing applications whether you want to use static or shared libraries. Here's a little more information to help you make that decision.

Shared libraries
If you use the shared libraries you will have to distribute some key DLLs (Dynamic Link Libraries) with your application in order to guarantee that it will run successfully on someone else's PC. In some cases (like the MFC DLLs) these libraries can be quite large.

However, this does mean that if the DLLs are updated for any reason you do not need to distribute your application again. Also, your application itself will be smaller because it uses the code in the DLLs instead of having its own copy of the code.

Static libraries

If you use the static libraries you will not have to distribute the runtime DLLs because your application has its own copy of the code that it uses in the libraries. However, your application will be larger as a result. Also, if the runtime DLLs are updated to fix any bugs you will have to re-compile your application with the new DLLs and redistribute it.

So, the choice is there if you need it. Deciding on one method or the other could save you another 52–64MB of disk space but more importantly it means that your development practices will be consistent.

REMEMBER

You will not be able to proceed if you do not have the latest version of Internet Explorer (which is supplied with Visual C++).

The setup process will also check the version of Internet Explorer that is running on your PC. If you do not have the latest version installed, setup will install it for you.

Once Visual C++ has been successfully installed you will be prompted to install MSDN (Microsoft Developer Network Library). You can either install the MSDN that comes with Visual C++, or if you are a MSDN subscriber you can install your MSDN subscription library at this point.

In order to access the online help you will obviously need to install the Visual C++ documentation. If you have enough disk space and you want to perform faster searches, then it is a good idea to install the full index search option as well.

You will also be asked if you want to install the InstallShield package that comes with Visual C++. If you are planning to develop commercial applications that you wish to distribute to customers then it is highly recommended that you install it. Otherwise, it is not really necessary.

What's New in Visual C++?

There are many new features in Visual C++ (far too many to mention here) but here is a look at some of the more interesting features – those that you are most likely to use on a day-to-day basis.

DHTML Viewing
You can now create applications that are capable of displaying Dynamic HTML pages.

New Common Controls
There are some new common controls for use in your applications. These include the IP address control, the date and time picker control and the calendar month control. These controls are also integrated into the Microsoft Foundation Classes which makes them easier for you to implement.

New and Updated MFCs
There are many new and updated MFCs with added functionality making it quicker and easier for you to develop applications.

HTML Help Workshop
For those of you not familiar with the HTML help workshop, it is what the new MSDN library and Visual C++ help systems are created with. You can now create your own HTML help packages for your applications. If you have a web site, these pages can be published without any conversion process to offer online help to your users.

Component Manager
Introduced to increase the support for code re-use, a major advantage of COMponent based applications.

InstallShield
The InstallShield product has been updated, making it easier for you to create installable packages for distribution to the users of your applications.

HTML Resources

You can now place HTML resources into your projects which, used in conjunction with the HTML viewing control, make it easier for you to develop professional looking user interfaces for your applications.

Edit and Continue Debugging

In the past, if you were debugging code and you altered any source code you would have to re-compile your whole application. Now you can edit the code and continue debugging without rebuilding your project.

IntelliSense

IntelliSense will help you to complete your code faster. For example, when you type the name of a function it pops up a small window showing you the parameters to that function without you having to look it up in the online help.

Dynamic Parsing

ClassView will automatically update your list of class members and functions while you are typing so you do not need to resave your project to see new functions.

New Project Types

There are some new project types in Visual C++. Also, some of the existing project types have been extended to include new features like creating Explorer-like applications and using Rebars instead of toolbars (Rebars are the toolbars seen in Internet Explorer).

Database support

The database support in Visual C++ has been greatly increased, especially with respect to web based applications that manipulate databases.

Sample Programs

There are many new sample programs to help you on your way with Visual C++.

General Improvements

The compiler and debugger have been made generally faster and more flexible.

Your First Look at Visual C++

Launch Visual C++ by selecting the icon from the Microsoft Visual C++ program group.

You should have a window that looks like the one shown below. There are some useful tools available in the Tools submenu but they perform very specific tasks and will be looked at in chapters that deal with their specific areas.

Workspace   Toolbar area

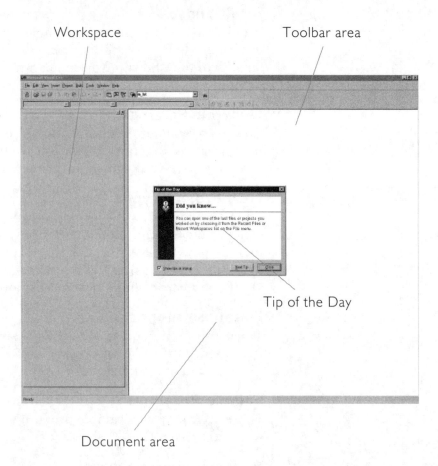

Tip of the Day

Document area

...cont'd

You can get tips at any time by selecting the Tip of the Day option in the Help menu.

Tip of the Day

Every time you start Visual C++ you will be given a handy tip about Visual C++. This option can be turned off by unchecking the check box and clicking Close.

Toolbar area

The menu and toolbars are placed in this area at the top of the window by default but they are 'dockable' anywhere around the edges of the Visual C++ window.

Workspace

The workspace is blank until a project is loaded, then it has three different functions: ClassView, ResourceView and FileView.

Document area

This is where you will spend most of your time. Source files and resources are loaded into this area when you edit them.

When you are editing source files in the editor, comments, keywords and strings are displayed in different colours to make it easier to identify typographical errors. The editor also supports many different file types including HTML files and VBS macros.

Changing What You See

You can reset the toolbars at any time, so don't be afraid to experiment.

Microsoft offer you many ways to change the look and feel of Visual C++. You can choose which toolbars are displayed and what is displayed on them. You can even create your own toolbars for a truly customised environment.

As with the menu and toolbars, the whole user interface of Visual C++ is made up of dockable windows that can be situated anywhere around the frame of the main window. The only exception to this is the status bar which is fixed at the bottom of the window.

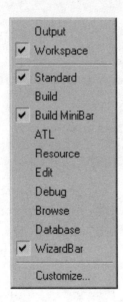

When you click the right mouse button on the toolbar area you are presented with the toolbar menu.

The majority of the toolbars are not displayed initially but can be shown (and hidden again) by simply selecting them from this list (the tick appears / disappears as appropriate).

You can also customize the toolbars by selecting the Customize option which allows you to decide which icons should appear on which toolbar(s).

You will notice there are two items at the top of this menu which are labelled Output and Workspace. These are not ordinary toolbars like the others although they are still dockable windows.

The Output window

If you click the box in the top-right corner of these windows they will close. But they can be retrieved from the menu shown above.

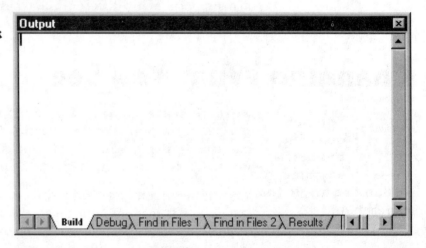

The Output window displays the output of various functions that Visual C++ performs. We will look at these in more detail when we come to use each particular function.

The Workspace window

At this point the Workspace window will be completely blank but once a project has been created/loaded it will look something like this:

You can easily dock these windows by double-clicking on the title bar.

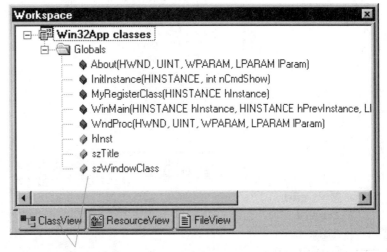

ClassView – displays information about the classes, functions and variables in your project.

You can go straight to the code of a function by double-clicking on the function name in the Workspace window.

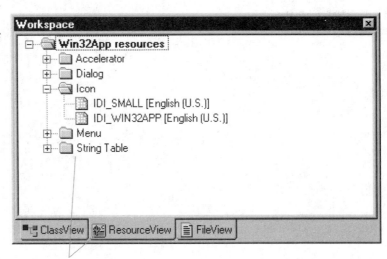

ResourceView – shows all of the resources in your application. Resources are things like icons, menus, bitmaps, dialog boxes, etc.

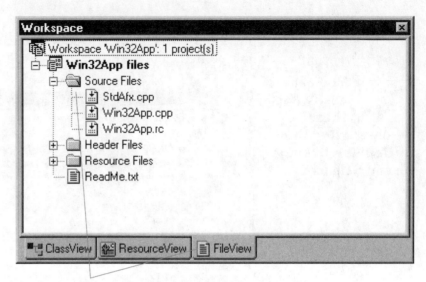

You can create your own folders in FileView which can contain any files you like. The files are categorised by their extensions.

FileView – displays the files that make up your project. FileView can have many folders which hold different types of files. For example, the Source Files folder contains all files that are compiled.

Well, that's the basic overview of the user interface. As you progress through this book you will learn more about the exciting features of Visual C++ and the many tasks that it can perform to make your code development quicker and easier.

Initially, many of the menu options and toolbar buttons are disabled but as you perform different tasks many more features will become available to you. Obviously, once you have started or loaded a project a lot more of these options will present themselves. This is what we will be doing in the next chapter.

Chapter Two

Your First Project

In this chapter we will look at the different project types that you can create with Visual C++ and then go on to actually create your first project.

Covers

Overview of Different Project Types

Visual C++ has many different project types to choose from which are all used for slightly different purposes.

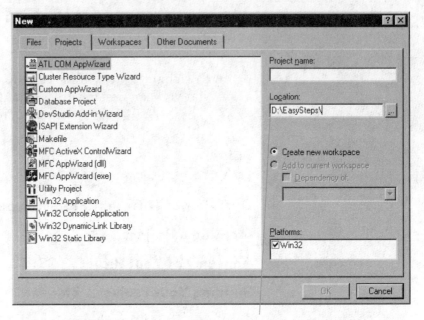

The folder which is displayed in the Location field initially is the starting point from which all of your projects are created. When you type in a project name, a subfolder is created beneath the Location folder.

You can have many projects in the same workspace, so if you already have a workspace open you can add the new project to the current workspace. This is useful is you are developing an application that has supporting DLLs. This way all related modules can be kept in one place. Otherwise a new workspace is created for your new project.

Here is a breakdown of what the different project types are, and what you might use them for:

ATL COM AppWizard

The Active Template Library (ATL) is a set of template based C++ classes which exist to make it easier for you to create COMponent based applications. The Component Object Model (COM) is a methodology introduced by Microsoft to encourage the re-use of code by splitting applications into smaller components.

Cluster Resource Type Wizard

A highly specialised kind of project which will generate an application which is cluster-aware.

Custom AppWizard

Allows you to create your own project type or extend the MFC project types. For example, you may want to create your own screen saver project type which contains the bulk of the work needed to create a screen saver application.

Database Project

Connects to a data source and gives you access to database tables. This type of project can be used in conjunction with InterDev for creating web solutions.

DevStudio Add-in Wizard

You can create add-ins for Visual C++ which will respond to certain events (such as opening a project) or certain keystrokes, enabling you to create an even more customised environment.

ISAPI Extension Wizard

Creates Internet Server Application Programming Interface filters which are used to extend Microsoft's Internet Information Server (IIS).

Makefile

This will create a very basic project which has no instructions for the compiler or linker. You will have to supply all of this information yourself.

MFC ActiveX ControlWizard

An ActiveX control is one which can be embedded in an ActiveX container such as Internet Explorer, Word, Excel or any other application that supports ActiveX (OLE).

MFC AppWizard (dll)

Creates a dynamic-link library which supports the Microsoft Foundation Classes. DLLs can contain code or just resources like icons, bitmaps, etc. This is essentially a Win32 DLL with the added functionality of MFC support.

 For quick applications use the MFC AppWizard project types. Most of the skeleton code is produced for you, saving time and effort.

MFC AppWizard (exe)

A Win32 application that supports the MFC. MFC applications are generally easier to construct but can be bigger because of the added functionality. Like the DLL project, this is simply a Win32 application which supports MFC.

Utility Project

A utility project does not create any executable code, it is used to store files that can be created without needing to be linked. For example, you may have a source file with some routines that you use regularly. Rather than having many copies of this source file, you can simply add a utility project containing your source file to each workspace in which you use it.

Win32 Application

Creates a Win32 application project with no MFC support. Win32 is the name for the 32-bit Windows platform which supports Windows 95, Windows 98 and Windows NT.

Win32 Console Application

This will create an application without MFC support which does not have a graphical interface. Instead it uses a console window similar to the MS-DOS prompt window. Console windows can be used for text only.

Win32 Dynamic-Link Library

A DLL which does not support the MFCs.

Win32 Static Library

Similar to a DLL but the output of this project is a static library (extension .LIB) which can be linked into other applications without having to distribute a DLL.

Creating a Project

By now you are probably itching to *actually* start programming. Good news! You are about to create your first project.

| Select New... from the File menu, or press Ctrl+N.

 If you change the Location field it will be remembered for future projects.

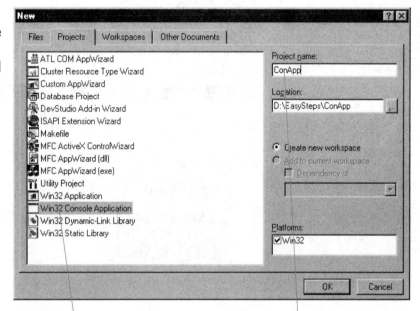

2 Choose the Win32 Console Application project type. At this point you may want to choose where to store all your projects.

3 Enter a name for your project. We'll call this first one ConApp.

4 Click OK to create the project.

You will now start choosing the options that you want to apply to your project.

A new folder has now been created for your project but your project has not actually been created, so if you want to choose another name or project type simply click '< Back' and you will be taken back to the previous screen.

You are now in a 1–step wizard. This project has few options (you have to go easy on your first project!). Other projects like the MFC projects have lots of different options for you to choose from which are presented in several stages via a wizard.

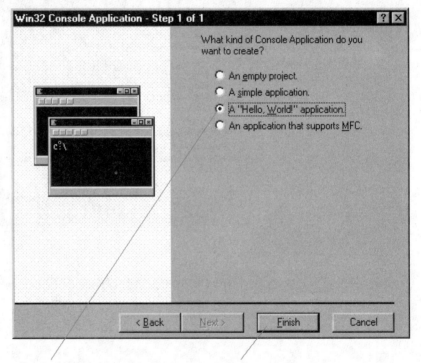

1 Select the 'A "Hello, World!" application' radio button.

2 Click Finish to complete the creation of your project.

There it is. You have now successfully created your first Visual C++ project. It's not very exciting admittedly but now you can start *really* getting to know Visual C++.

Anatomy of Your Project

Visual C++ should now look something like this:

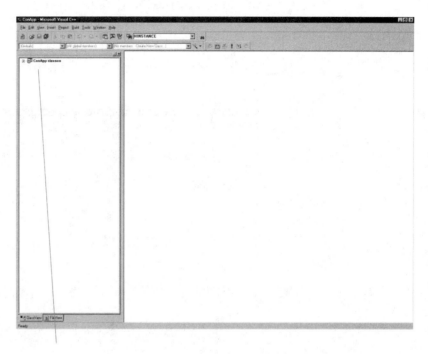

You will see that the Workspace window now contains some information about your project.

You may remember from earlier that you can go straight to the code for a function by double-clicking on the function name in ClassView.

This project only has one function which is the 'main' function. The main function is what we call the entry-point for your program. This is where you take over what your program does when it is loaded and when this function is finished the program has ended.

You are now going to look at the main function. It doesn't do very much in this project but it gives you an idea about how a program should be structured.

The quickest way to view a function is to double-click on the function in ClassView.

1 Expand ConApp classes by clicking on the box with a + symbol (or double-clicking the text).

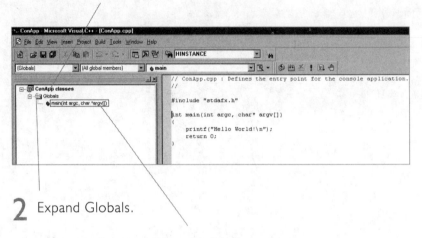

2 Expand Globals.

3 Double-click on the main function.

This will locate the source code file that contains the code for the main function and load it into the document editing area of Visual C++.

As you can see, the main function is very simple. It only performs one task: displaying "Hello World!" on the screen.

Look at the line of code where it does this. You will see that main executes another function called 'printf'. As you may have guessed, printf is a function for printing information. However, this is not printing in the way that you would use a laser printer but it is printing to the screen.

The next line of code simply 'returns' a value of zero. The value that your program returns can be an indication of whether the program was successful in its operation.

Remember that once the main function returns, your program has finished executing. The return value from your main function is also known as the program's 'exit code'.

The exit code can be checked by the program that executed your program. For instance, in a batch file the variable 'errorlevel' is used to check the exit code of a program

There are some other keywords that are used in this source code but you do not need to worry about these for now. This project is just to show you the basic structure of a project and what the Workspace window looks like with something actually in it.

You have now created a project but you have not actually created a program. If you want to see this code in action, you are going to have to generate an executable program from your source code files.

To create an executable, you need to compile all the source code files into object files, compile any resources and then link all of your objects with any runtime libraries that your code uses.

To save you having to perform all of these steps, Visual C++ supplies you with a single process. One function will perform all of these steps in one go making it easier for you to create applications.

Building Your Project

Select Build ConApp.exe from the Build menu (F7).

This program will only be executable on Win32 platforms.

That's all you have to do! Now, the source files will be compiled into machine code modules and linked with some standard code which manages the loading of your application to produce an executable program.

You will notice that the Output window is now displayed automatically. This is so that you can see what is happening during the building of your application. If there are any errors or warnings during the build they will be displayed here.

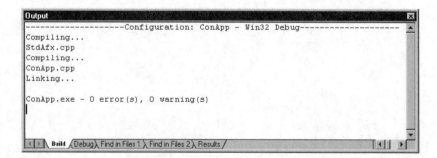

Your Output window should contain the above.

Changing Build Configurations

You may have noticed the first line of the Output window. It states that the current build configuration is Win32 Debug. This means that your program can be debugged using the Visual C++ debugger.

If you look at the Build menu you will notice that there is a Start Debug submenu. This will start your program in the debugger so that you can debug any problems that you may have. You can insert breakpoints that will stop your program at a certain line of code and watch variables to see what happens to them as your code executes. We will take a more detailed look at debugging later on.

If you are satisfied that your code is bug-free, you can build a release version which is a lot smaller and faster than the debug version.

To change the current build configuration:

A separate folder is created for each build configuration so you can switch between debug and release easily without having to rebuild your project.

| Select Set Active Configuration from the Build menu.

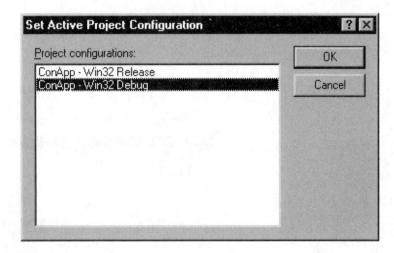

There are usually two build configurations supplied by the AppWizard but you can create more if you have more specialised needs. For example, you may want two different versions of your program, one for Windows 98 and one for Windows NT.

Another way to change your build configuration is to change the toolbars that Visual C++ displays.

If you right-click on the toolbar area you will notice that there are two choices for the build toolbar: 'Build' and 'Build MiniBar'.

The 'Build' bar contains a drop-down list of the configurations available for your project which makes it easier to switch between configurations.

Active Project   Active configuration

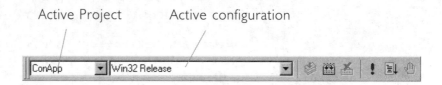

Project Settings

As well as changing the type of application that you are going to build, you can also change many other aspects of your project.

Select Settings from the Project menu (ALT+F7).

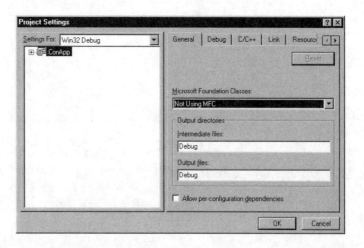

The tabs in this dialog enable you to change many different things about your project. Most of the options in these tabs do not need to be changed very often (if at all).

The settings are changed for the current build configuration that you have active. You can change the build configuration for which you are changing the settings by selecting it from the drop down list labelled 'Settings For:'.

Generally, it is not recommended to change many of these options unless you know what you are doing. However, sometimes it is necessary for you to change these settings yourself.

When you build your project, Visual C++ links many libraries of functions into your application for you. These are known as the 'default libraries'.

If you want to use additional functions from other software development kits (SDKs) supplied by Microsoft or a third party provider, you will have to instruct Visual C++ to link those libraries into your application.

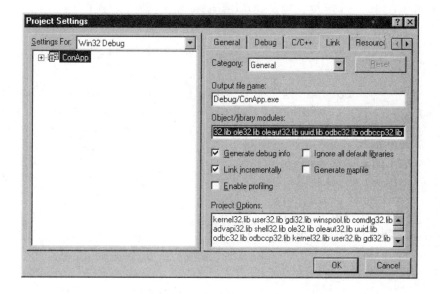

In the 'Link' tab there is a field labelled 'Object/library modules:'. This field contains a list of additional libraries that will be linked to your application.

If you run your application within Visual C++ for debugging purposes, you can also change the starting directory for the application (in case it needs to access files) and the arguments that are passed to the program.

There are some very advanced settings in the 'C/C++' and 'Link' tabs which change parameters that are passed to the compiler and linker. You should not really change these unless you know what you are doing, although they probably will not cause any adverse effect.

If you change any of the settings that affect the way your program is built, you will be prompted by Visual C++ to rebuild any files that were affected by your changes.

Executing Your Program

Assuming that everything has gone smoothly up until this point, and there were no errors with building ConApp, you should now have an executable program.

Select Execute ConApp from the Build menu. (F5)

REMEMBER

ConApp is a console application and thus should really be run from an MS-DOS prompt. If you run it from Windows it will disappear very quickly.

You will see an MS-DOS style window which contains "Hello World!". It also prompts you to press a key to continue. This is put there by Visual C++ (otherwise the program would just disappear again because it has finished at this point).

The program will reside in the output folder for your current configuration.

You have now created and executed your first program with Visual C++. The application that you execute from within Visual C++ is a file with the .exe extension which is the final output of your project. This means that the executable file is now ready for distribution.

When you build your project, Visual C++ creates a folder under the one which contains your project. If you have built a debug application the folder is called Debug and likewise Release when you create a release build.

When you are ready to distribute your application, create a release version. Apart from being a smaller executable, it will use DLLs that may already exist on somebody else's PC so you won't need to distribute them.

What Happens Behind the Scenes?

Earlier we looked at what happens when you build your project. The source code files are compiled, then linked with the Visual C++ runtime code to create an executable (or DLL).

To appreciate fully what is happening though, you really need to know what is happening behind the scenes.

Before the niceties of the IDE and Visual Studio as we know it today, things were very different when it came to creating programs. There were no nice graphical editors which changed the colours for keywords and no integrated editing, compiling and debugging environment.

Visual C++ is really a front-end for some command line programs which do the guts of the work in creating your program. CL.EXE and LINK.EXE are the compiler and linker that create your programs.

The stages of program production go something like this:

Preprocessing
The preprocessor is a special program which runs through the source code before it is even looked at by the compiler. The preprocessor is responsible for including external files into your source and resolving symbolic names into their integral values. Special directives are given to the preprocessor by using the #-prefixed keywords such as #include and #define.

#include tells the preprocessor to include another file at that point in the source code. Being able to include other files allows you to store common code in separate files and it breaks your source code down into smaller portions.

REMEMBER

There are many other preprocessor directives but these are the most commonly used.

#define will tell the preprocessor that a meaningful name actually refers to a numerical value so that you can use MAX_PATH in your code instead of 260 which means nothing.

Compiling

Each of the source files in your project are passed (along with many parameters) on the command line to CL.EXE which compiles the source code into an object file (file extension .obj) which is machine readable.

The object files are intermediate files which means that they are not needed once your final application has been built.

Linking

All of your object files are then linked together along with some runtime code as mentioned before. External references are also resolved at this point. An external reference is a reference to a function or a variable that is not declared within your source code files.

Nearly all of the functions that you use are external to your source code files. Visual C++ prevents you from having to know which libraries they are in by linking a default set of libraries with your application (SHELL32, KERNEL32, etc.) which you are most likely to use.

If you use any functions from third-party developers you will have to specify to Visual C++ where the functions can be found.

As long as each of these stages are successful you will end up with an executable program.

Files That Make Up a Project

There are many different file types that make up an entire project. Some of them are project files that tell Visual C++ what options apply to your project, others are source code files to be included in your project.

The following files are created for every project. They are project based files which specify options and layouts, etc.

project.dsw	project workspace file
project.dsp	project file
project.opt	project options file
project.ncb	program database
readme.txt	information about the project

There are various source files that can be included in projects:

source.cpp	main source code file
source.h	main header file
project.rc	resource script
project.odl	object definition language

There may be extra source and header files depending on the kind of project that you create.

The following intermediate files are created when you build your project and can be deleted when you have finished the development of your project. It is useful to keep these files while you are still developing your project because they reduce the amount of time that it takes to build your output.

project.ilk	linker database
source.obj	compiled source code module
project.pch	precompiled header
vc60.idb	program database
project.res	compiled resources

There are different output file types which are dependent upon the type of project that you create:

project.exe	executable application
project.dll	dynamic link library
project.ocx	ActiveX control
project.lib	static code library
project.tlb	type library for ActiveX control

Generally, source files that have the '.c' extension are C source files whereas files with the '.cpp' extension are C++ source files.

Header files have the extension '.h', '.hpp' or '.hxx'. They are all header files that can be included with #include.

Source files and header files are compiled together to generate object files (.obj).

Resource scripts (.rc) can also include header files and are compiled to generate files with a .res extension.

All of the object files for your project are then linked with the resources (if applicable) and as many libraries as necessary to ensure that all references are resolved.

This certainly covers the most commonly used file types. There may be others that are not covered here but they are only used in special project types.

The C++ Language

This chapter will explain some of the basic concepts of the C/C++ Language and should enable you to go on to write your own programs.

Chapter Three

Covers

Variable Types and Ranges

Now that you have created your first project, it's back to some theory.

Computers were designed to manipulate data so it makes sense to look at the different data types at your disposal.

C++ has a limited number of data types, each of which is a different size. Each data type occupies a fixed amount of memory and thus has limits to the values that it can contain.

There are two groups of data types that are supported by C++.

Integral Data Types

char	(1 byte)
short	(2 bytes)
int	(4 bytes on a 32-bit platform)
long	(4 bytes)

Unsigned variables can hold twice as much information as signed variables but must be positive.

These data types are signed by default which means that they can have a positive or a negative value. This can be altered by prefixing any of these data types with the keyword 'unsigned'.

Floating-point Data Types

float	(4 bytes)
double	(8 bytes)

Floating-point data types are used to store decimal numbers. For example, PI (3.141592).

Different data types should be used for different purposes – eg, 'chars' are used to store alphanumeric characters and other keyboard characters (!"£$% etc.).

The different data types have different sizes and can therefore hold different maximum values. The following table shows the various data types and their value ranges.

...cont'd

 REMEMBER

Use variable types that suit your needs. For example, there is no point in using an __int64 when storing a person's age.

Type	Range of Values
__int8	-128 to 127
__int16	-32,768 to 32,767
__int32	-2,147,483,648 to 2,147,483,647
__int64	-9,223,372,036,854,775,808 to 9,223,372,036,854,775,807
char	-128 to 127
unsigned char	0 to 255
short	-32,768 to 32,767
unsigned short	0 to 65,535
long	-2,147,483,648 to 2,147,483,647
unsigned long	0 to 4,294,967,295
float	3.4E +/- 38 (7 digits)
double	1.7E +/- 308 (15 digits)
long double	1.2E +/- 4932 (19 digits)

You will notice that unsigned variables can hold much bigger values than signed variables, approximately twice as much. However, they can only hold positive values.

Defining Your Own Variable Types

You can create synonyms for existing data types by using the keyword 'typedef' (an abbreviation of *type definition*) which allows you to define new data types.

By using the typedef keyword, a variable of data type long can also be represented as LONG or LPARAM. This is the case in Windows, many of the data types you will encounter are type definitions based on one of the above types.

These synonyms are resolved by the compiler into their original type when compiling your code so there is no speed deficit when using them. It may seem pointless to use typedef to create new names for existing data types but sometimes it can make code easier to understand.

REMEMBER

Type definitions do not introduce new variable types, just new names for existing variable types.

Type definitions have the following syntax:

    typedef *existing-type synonym*;

You may want to create a synonym for the unsigned long variable type called 'ulong'. This would mean a lot less typing if you had a program that uses a lot of unsigned long variables. Your type definition would look like this:

    typedef unsigned long ulong;

If you do use type definitions, be careful when debugging your code because Visual C++ *decodes* your type definition so that it knows exactly which variable type you are using. This way, it knows how much memory to allocate for your variables. As a result, Visual C++ may tell you that your variable is a different type to what you think it should be.

Declaring Variables

In order to use these data types, you need to declare variables in your code. You can declare variables in the following way:

    variable-type variable-name;

This will tell Visual C++ that you want to set aside enough memory to hold your new variable.

The variable types mentioned in the previous table are all recognised keywords in Visual C++ and will appear in a different colour when you type them in.

However, if you are using a variable type defined with the typedef keyword it will not appear in a different colour. Do not be alarmed: this is just because the editor doesn't know about your defined type.

All of the variables that are declared in your program must have a unique name so that Visual C++ can assign each variable to a specific memory address.

...cont'd

If you had two variables with the same name, Visual C++ wouldn't know which one you were referring to when you updated it.

There are many recommendations for naming conventions when declaring variables. It is a good idea to adopt a naming standard so that when someone else looks at your code they can easily see the types of variables without having to find their declaration in the code.

Here are some suggested prefixes for different data types:

Variable type	Prefix
char	c
short	s
int	n
long	l
float	f
double	d

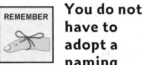 **You do not have to adopt a naming convention, it is just a recommendation.**

So, if you have a **char**acter variable that contains a person's age, the variable would be declared thus:

```
char cAge;
```

You can declare many variables of the same type by separating them with a comma:

```
char cAge, cHeight, cWeight;
```

You do not need to declare one variable per line.

Variable names must begin with an alphabetic character – they cannot begin with a number.

Assigning Values to Variables

Assigning a value to a variable is basically common sense. If you have a variable called 'nAge', and you want to assign the value 21 to that variable, you would enter the following code:

```
nAge = 21;
```

If you want to assign a letter to a character variable you can enclose the letter in single quotes, for example:

```
cEss = 's';
```

The only exception to this is when you have a line of text. In programming terms a line of text is called a 'string'. You may have noticed that there isn't a variable type to hold strings.

If you think about it, a string is just a collection of characters, so to assign a value to a string involves assigning values to many characters.

A string is also called a character 'array'.

Arrays of Variables

Sometimes one variable just isn't enough. Suppose you want to store the ages of ten different people, you would have to declare ten uniquely named variables.

This makes things look untidy, gives you more variable names to remember and also makes it more complicated to perform operations on these variables.

To get around these problems, you can have what is called an array of variables. An array of variables is probably best described as a 'row' of variables.

An array of variables can contain a huge number of *elements*. An element is a single variable within the array.

Each element in an array is as big as the type of the variable that the array contains. So, each element in a character array occupies one byte of memory (the size of a character).

...cont'd

Arrays are declared like this:

variable-type array-name[*number-of-elements*];

Variable type
Can be any variable type including any synonyms declared using typedef.

Array name
The name of an array has the same restrictions (and naming convention recommendations) as single variables.

A text string is an array of characters. The number of elements in the array is the length of the string.

Number of elements
The number of elements in an array dictates how many variables are contained within the array.

The square brackets that enclose the number of elements must be included in the declaration. They do not denote an optional entry.

Once you have an array of variables, you need to know how to access individual elements of the array.

The elements in the array are zero-based which basically means that the first element in the array is number zero.

To retrieve an element from an array, use the array name followed by the element that you wish to retrieve (zero based) enclosed in square brackets.

For example:

```
char cAges[10];
```

Declares an array which contains the ages of ten people.

```
cAges[2] = 21;
```

Would tell the compiler to store the value 21 in the third element of the cAges array.

Some Pointers About Memory

The primary storage medium of a computer is memory and every variable (no matter what type) has an associated 'memory address'.

All variables declared in your source code are of a fixed size and space is allocated in the executable file for them. This means that the amount of memory that these variables are allowed to use cannot change while the program is running.

Supposing you want to store some numbers, but when you are writing your code you do not know how many numbers there will be. How do you cater for this? Do you declare an array and hope that it will be big enough?

When you declare a pointer, no memory has been allocated so the contents of the pointer will be invalid. Trying to access this pointer will result in a page fault.

Think of the problems that this could introduce. What if your array isn't big enough? You would have to increase the size of your array, re-compile your program and redistribute it . . . not very professional!

If you were to use a 'pointer', you could allocate as much memory as you need while the program is running instead of fixing the amount when you write your code.

When your program is loaded, memory is allocated for variables and the variable is associated with the address of the allocated memory. Pointers are therefore more complicated to implement because you have to handle the allocation and deallocation of memory yourself.

To declare a pointer, use the following syntax:

variable-type *pointer-name;

Variable type
The variable type can be any of the data types that we have discussed.

Pointer name
The name that you assign to the pointer is a variable name and so must conform to the same conventions as regular variable names.

...cont'd

REMEMBER

A pointer contains the memory address of information, not the information itself.

When using the pointer in code, you are referring to the actual memory address that the pointer points to. However, the data itself is actually contained *within* that memory address.

To access the contents of the memory that the pointer is pointing to, you need to 'dereference' the pointer. This is done by prefixing the pointer name with an asterisk.

Dereferencing a pointer tells the compiler that you want to look at the contents of the memory address that the pointer points to rather than the memory address itself.

Sometimes you need to supply a pointer to a variable. Rather than declaring a pointer, allocating memory and initialising it you can use the 'ampersand' (&) operator.

The ampersand operator tells the compiler to use the memory address of a variable rather than the value that a variable contains.

Managing Your Memory

When you first declare a pointer, it is given an arbitrary value and hence does not point to a valid block of memory. Before you can use the pointer you must allocate some memory and assign the address of the allocated memory to the pointer.

The new operator

You can allocate memory by using the 'new' operator. The new operator *returns* a pointer to a memory address which you can then assign to your pointer.

The code below demonstrates how to declare a pointer and assign it to a block of allocated memory:

```
int *pAge;

pAge = new int;
```

...cont'd

BEWARE

If you change the value of a pointer, you will lose the block of memory associated with the pointer, resulting in a memory leak.

The size of an 'int'eger is four bytes so the above statement (page 43) will allocate a block of memory four bytes long and assign the address of that block of memory to the pointer pAge.

If you do not free the memory that you allocate, the memory will remain allocated when your program finishes, resulting in a memory leak. Too many of these and your system will start grinding to a halt.

Allocating arrays dynamically

The name of an array is associated with the memory address of the start of the array, so it is, in effect, a pointer.

Arrays can be allocated dynamically by using the same convention with the 'new' operator as used when declaring an array:

```
int *pAges;

pAges = new int[10];
```

This would dynamically allocate enough memory for ten integers (40 bytes).

To avoid memory leaks you must deallocate any memory that you have allocated with the 'new' operator.

This is done by using the 'delete' operator.

To free a single block of memory (not allocated as an array) you simply delete the pointer:

```
delete pAge;
```

To delete a block of memory that was allocated as an array, use the following syntax:

```
delete [] pAges;
```

Make sure that you always free as much memory as you allocate and you should have no memory leaks.

Function Declarations

Functions are the building blocks of any programming language. You use functions to manipulate data and report the results of the manipulation.

In C++ functions are declared in the following way:

return-type function-name(*argument-list*);

Let's look at each part of the function declaration in turn.

Return type

The return type specifies the data type that this function will pass back to its caller. Any data type can be specified as a return type as well as a special return type: 'void'. The void data type has no type and has no size. When using the void return type you are basically telling the compiler that the function will not return any data.

REMEMBER

There should be white space between the return type and the function name.

Function name

The name of a function is an identifier that the compiler associates with a block of code, in the same way it does with variables. Whenever you call a function, the compiler jumps to the block of code associated with that function name and starts executing it.

Argument list

A function can take any number of arguments. The arguments are enclosed in parentheses and are separated by commas. If your function takes no parameters you can insert the keyword void but this is assumed by the compiler if the parentheses are empty.

Arguments can also be called 'formal parameters'.

Finally, the declaration is terminated by a semi-colon character.

A function declaration only tells the compiler that the function exists, it does not contain the instructions that the function executes. Just like variable declarations tell the compiler that the variable exists, but they do not assign a value to the variable.

Function Definitions

A function definition tells the compiler what a function actually does. A function definition looks something like this.

return-type function-name(*argument-list*)

{

    statements

}

HANDY TIP

Make your function names meaningful to what they do. When you come back to code after several months it can be confusing if your function names do not make sense.

You will notice that the function definition is very similar to a function declaration, with the following differences.

The function definition is not terminated by a semi-colon but is instead followed by an opening curly bracket ({) which designates the start of a code block.

A closing curly bracket (}) designates the end of the function block.

Between the curly brackets can be any number of 'statements'.

Statements can be variable definitions, function calls, arithmetic operations. Anything that constitutes compilable code.

Before calling any function, you must have declared its existence to the compiler so that the compiler knows which memory address to jump to when you call the function.

In order to use functions in external libraries such as 'printf' (in ConApp) you need to have declarations for them.

This is why you need to include header files for the standard C/C++ libraries. These header files declare functions so that they can be called from your code without any complaints from the compiler.

Although you can declare variables outside of a function, all executable code must be contained within a function.

Controlling the Flow of Execution

Declaring functions and variables is all well and good but what do you do with them once you have them?

The flow of a program is synchronous, that is, it follows one 'thread' of execution. The program starts at the beginning of the main function; the main function then calls other functions but does not carry on until those functions return.

However, you do not always want all of your code to execute, you may want to only execute certain parts of your code if certain conditions are met.

There are basically two ways of altering the flow of execution of a program: jumping to other sections of code, and branching into different sections of code.

Jumping around

There are three keywords which are used to jump to alternative sections of code: 'goto', 'return' and 'break'. (Although, strictly speaking, 'return' simply returns from a function rather than actually jumping to another section of code).

You can 'return' from a function at any time. In fact this is how most functions indicate a failure, by returning a different value than they would in a successful situation.

Remember to free all memory that you have allocated before returning prematurely from a function.

Sometimes you do not want to return from a function but you do not want to execute some code, so you can use 'goto' to jump to a specified label. Labels are declared by specifying a name followed by a colon (:).

The 'break' keyword will break out of a section of code. Remember that sections of code are surrounded by curly brackets.

Branching out

You won't always want to return prematurely from a function. The other alternative is to use 'logical operators'.

REMEMBER

You do not always need an 'else' clause with your 'if' statements.

The 'if' and 'else' keywords can be used to check *if* an expression is *true*. The syntax is as follows:

```
if (expression) {

    statements

} [ else {

    statements

} ]
```

It all makes sense really, *if* an expression is true a certain set of statements are executed *else* another set are executed.

This is all well and good for comparing two values, but what if you want to compare a value against several values? This could be done with several if statements but would look a lot neater with a 'switch' statement.

This is the syntax of a switch:

```
switch (expression) {

    case constant:

        statements

        break;

    default:

        break;

}
```

You can have any number of case statements within your switch statement, each one comparing a different constant value with the expression.

...cont'd

The 'default' statement captures any matches that have not been catered for by the case statements.

Let's look at what can make up an expression for these flow manipulators.

Expressions

Expressions can be a single value or a relational check. Expressions resulting in a value of zero are considered to be 'false'; anything else is 'true'.

Relational operators compare two values and result in a true or false condition. They are called binary operators because they perform their operations on two values.

These are the relational operators provided by C++:

a < b	a is less than b.
a <= b	a is less than (or equal to) b.
a > b	a is greater than b.
a >= b	a is greater than (or equal to) b.
a == b	a is equal to b.
a != b	a is not equal to b.

These operators can be used on any values, whether they are variables, pointers or return values from functions.

There are other operators that manipulate variables which can also be used in conjunction with the tests involved in 'if' and 'switch' statements:

Increment/decrement

++	increment
--	decrement

The increment and decrement operators can be used before or after a variable name. As you may suspect by their names, these operators will increase and decrease the value of a variable by one respectively.

If they are used before a variable, the value is changed before its value is used. If they are used after the variable the value of the variable is used, then changed.

Mathematical operators

There are operators available for most of the simple mathematical functions that you can perform in every day life. The more complex mathematical procedures require a function.

Some of the mathematical operators are the same as those you would use in everyday life (ie, '+' for addition, '-' for subtraction and '/' for division). But others are not the same:

*	multiplication
%	modulus

Logical operators are also useful for performing multiple checks. For example, to validate a value entered by a user for the hour, the value must be greater than zero AND less than twenty three.

||	OR
!	NOT
&&	AND

This is not all of the operators but it's certainly enough to perform most mathematical and logical operations.

Looping

Another useful form of flow control is looping. You may want to perform a set of statements multiple times without having to use goto labels and checking variables.

There are three mechanisms that can be used to repeat operations. Each has a different way of controlling the loop.

Loops can be broken out of at any point by using the break keyword.

The *for* loop

```
for (initialise; condition; loop) {

        statements

}
```

As you can see, there are three parts to the for loop, separated by semi-colon characters.

Initialise
Before the loop actually starts, the initialise statement is executed which is used to initialise the loop variable.

Condition
The condition statement is checked after every iteration of the loop. Once the condition is false, the loop terminates.

Loop
Once the condition has been checked and results in a true value, the loop statement should update the loop variable(s).

Another post-condition loop is the do-while loop. The do-while loop basically says "do all these statements while this value is not true".

```
do {

        statements

} while (condition);
```

This is similar to the 'for' loop except for the fact that the initialisation is not part of the loop. However, the mechanism is identical.

The final loop is the 'while' loop which is a pre-condition loop. It is so-called because the condition is checked *before* each iteration of the loop.

```
while (condition) {

    statements

}
```

If the condition results in a 'false' value on the first check, the loop may never even be entered at all. The loop is repeated *while* condition is 'true'.

Structures

You may have a number of variables that are all related in some way, for example you may have variables for a persons name, age, address, telephone number, etc. These variables can be put together into another data type called a structure.

Structures are defined with the keyword 'struct':

```
struct tag {

    members

};
```

REMEMBER **If you use 'typedef' (type defined) data types in a structure, the type definition must appear before it is used in the structure.**

The members of a struct can be any kind of data type, even your own type definitions. A structure to hold information about a location on the screen may look something like this:

```
struct CELL {

    int x;

    int y;

    COLORREF clr;
};
```

...cont'd

This would create a structure called CELL which contains the (x,y) co-ordinates and the colour of a screen location.

This structure could then be used as a data type, so you can declare instances of it, arrays of it and pointer to it.

Structures are also declared with the keyword struct:

   struct *tag variable-name*;

Here are some example declarations:

   struct CELL MyCell;

   struct CELL *pMyCell;

   struct CELL MyCells[20];

Accessing structure members

How to access the individual members of a structure depends on how the structure was declared.

If the structure was declared as a regular variable (as in the first instance above) then the members are accessed by using the following notation:

   variable-name.member

The full stop character tells Visual C++ that you want to access a member of the structure. This is where a neat feature of Visual C++ comes into play: IntelliSense.

When you access a member of a structure, just after you press the full stop key, you will be prompted to choose the member that you wish to access.

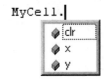

You can carry on typing or select the member that you want to access from the list displayed.

If you want to access a member of structure through a pointer to that structure, the notation is slightly different:

variable-name-> member

This tells Visual C++ to 'de-reference' the pointer before accessing the member of the structure. IntelliSense will still work on pointers to structures.

Functions can also be stored in structures but they must still be unique throughout the modules in your application. If you want to create self-contained objects which have member functions as well as member variables, you can use classes.

Classes

C++ classes are declared with the 'class' keyword.

Classes (if designed properly) can be thought of as self-contained objects that contain their own data and their own functions that manipulate this data.

The member functions of a class are not limited to operating on data members. They are functions, the same as any other.

Class Definition
A class definition looks something like this.

```
class class-name [: base-class(es)]

{


};
```

Class name
The name of a class becomes a data type of which you declare variables. Just as you would with an 'int' or 'char'.

Base class(es)
One of the key characteristics of classes is that they can be 'derived' from other classes. Derivation is where one class is based upon another and thus 'inherits' its base classes functionality.

...cont'd

A class definition also has curly brackets to symbolise the beginning and end of the class but they do not surround a code block in this instance.

A class usually has three sections: construction/destruction, implementation and data members.

Construction/destruction

A class's constructor is a function which has the same name as the class it is constructing. A constructor is the same as a normal function except that it 'cannot' have a return type. The destructor for a class has the same name as the class but is prefixed with a tilde character (~). Destructors are not allowed any arguments either.

When you declare a variable that is of your class type, the constructor is called as part of the instantiation of that variable. Similarly, when the class variable is destroyed the destructor is called as part of the cleanup.

Implementation

The implementation of a class is the set of member functions that will perform operations on the data members of that class.

Data members

The data that is associated with this class. In order to create self-contained classes they should be designed in such a way that any information relating to them is contained within the class. For example, if you had a class that encompassed time, its data members would probably consist of three character data members (for hours, minutes and seconds).

To ensure the integrity of your data, you can prevent other functions from accessing the data members of a class by applying access restrictions.

You will learn more about classes when you start to use the MFC.

Restricting Access to Your Members

There are three access specifiers that you can use when describing to the compiler how to treat the members of your classes: public, private and protected.

Public members

Public members are available to any functions in your code whether they are members of the class or not.

Private members

Private members are private to the class in which they are defined. Even classes derived from the class do not have access to them and functions that aren't a member of the class certainly don't have access to them!

Protected members

These members are protected by the abstraction that classes provide. Member functions of the class can access protected members freely, as can members of derived classes. However, functions that are external to this class cannot.

When an access specifier is used, all members adopt that security attribute until another access specifier is used.

And what is derivation? You may have a class that provides a lot of functionality that you want to use again but in a slightly different way. What you can do is to 'derive' a new class from the existing class.

When you derive a class from another, the derived class 'inherits' all of the members of its 'base class'. But you can also add to the new class extending the functionality of the base class.

Well, those are the basics of the C++ language. With the contents of this chapter you should have enough information to create simple C++ programs.

However, you probably bought this book with Windows programming in mind, so let's look at Windows!

Basic Windows

In this chapter you will learn about the structure of Windows programs. You will create a simple Windows program which demonstrates the topics talked about in this chapter.

Chapter Four

Covers

A Quick Look at Windows Programs

Visual programming is all about programming under Windows, right? So let's look at how programs are constructed under Windows.

A new entry point

A program running under Windows is the same as any other program . . . well, almost. It has an entry point the same as other programs, although it is slightly different in its declaration:

```
int WINAPI WinMain(

    HINSTANCE hInstance,

    HINSTANCE hPreviousInstance,

    LPTSTR lpszCmdLine,

    int nCmdShow);
```

Another key difference with Windows applications is that of the message queue. Every thread that executes under Windows has an associated message queue. Messages are placed into the queue by the Windows system, other applications or your own application.

Messages

The main part of a Windows program is the 'message loop'. The message loop takes messages out of the front of the queue and passes them to the 'message handler'. The message handler is responsible for handling the various messages that are sent to your application.

Messages are used for almost everything in Windows applications to notify you that things must be done, or that things have just happened. You can also define your own messages for custom operations/notifications.

You can see an example of what these functions look like by creating a 'Win32 Application' project in Visual C++. This is what we will do now so that you can visualise what we are talking about in this chapter.

Creating a Windows Program

Now, create a simple Windows program.

I   Select New from the File Menu.

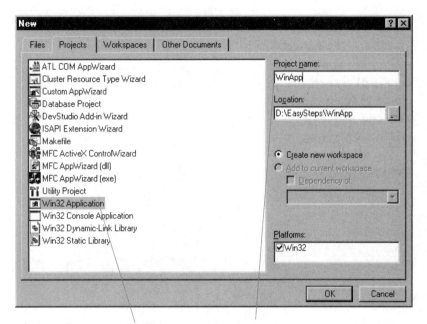

2   Choose the 'Win32 Application' project type.

3   Type WinApp as the project name.

4   Click 'OK'.

This will start the Win32 Application AppWizard which will prompt you for the type of project that you wish to create.

Select 'A typical "Hello World!" application' and click 'Finish'. The AppWizard will now create a Windows application project for you and will generate the necessary code for a simple Windows application with a message loop and some other startup code.

If you expand all of the levels in the FileView (in the Workspace window) you will see that the project that was generated for you by AppWizard has the following files:

Using projects that are generated by AppWizard are a good way to get started quickly without having to write similar code in every project.

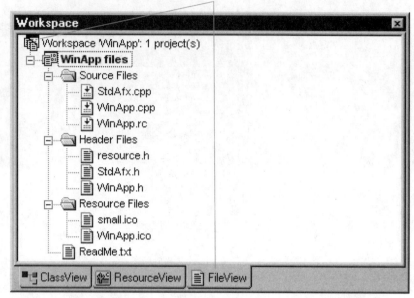

WinApp.cpp is the main source code file for your project. It contains the WinMain function and the message loop mentioned earlier.

The generated project also performs some other standard operations that all Windows applications need in order to function properly. For example, if you are to display a window, it must be created in the proper fashion. This is done in the 'InitInstance' function.

Some global variables are defined for you in this source file:

HINSTANCE hInst;

TCHAR szTitle[MAX_LOADSTRING];

TCHAR szWindowClass[MAX_LOADSTRING];

It was mentioned earlier that in Windows many data types appear differently. Well, here are two examples.

...cont'd

REMEMBER

The compiler does not always use the correct types when reporting errors. It sometimes uses the base data types.

TCHAR can be defined as two different data types depending on the type of project you are creating.

If you create an ANSI project, 'TCHAR' is defined as 'CHAR', which in turn is defined as 'char'.

If your project supports Unicode then TCHAR is defined as 'WCHAR' which is defined as 'short'.

'HINSTANCE' is defined as a 'void *'.

You do not need to worry about the base data types that the Windows data types are defined as, just as long as you use the correct types in the correct places.

What are these variables used for?

Here is a brief description of what these variables are used for:

hInstance   Contains a handle to the instance of your application. This is used for application specific operations like loading resources. A handle is just another pointer.

szTitle   The title of your window.

szWindowClass   The name of the window class associated with your window.

These variables are defined globally so that they are available anywhere in your program. The message loop and WinMain are two different functions so any variables that may want to be shared between them must be global.

As well as these variables, there are also some functions declared for you which perform the operations needed to get your application up and running:

```
ATOM      MyRegisterClass(HINSTANCE);

BOOL      InitInstance(HINSTANCE, int);
```

```
LRESULT CALLBACK WndProc(

    HWND,

    UINT,

    WPARAM,

    LPARAM);

LRESULT CALLBACK About(

    HWND,

    UINT,

    WPARAM,

    LPARAM);
```

These functions each perform a key stage of the initialisation process for your application. Here's what they do:

MyRegisterClass	Registers a window class for your application window. Window classes are described in more detail later on.
InitInstance	Initialises this instance of your application by creating and displaying a window. The class registered in MyRegisterClass is used to create the window.
WndProc	This is the message handler for the window created in InitInstance.
About	Handles the messages for a dialog box which displays information about your application.

If you build and execute the program generated by this project you will see all of these steps come together in an application that creates and displays a window.

62 **Visual C++ in easy steps**

Seeing Your Windows Program

Building a Windows program (in fact any program) is the same as building ConApp from Chapter 2:

Click the Build icon, select Build from the Build menu or press F7.

Then execute WinApp:

Click on the Execute icon, select Execute from the Build menu or press F5.

... and you will have a window that looks like this:

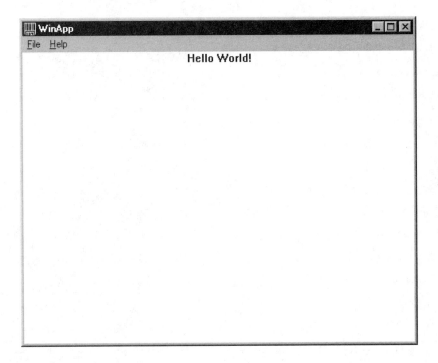

Your first Windows application. Now let's have a look at how all this is achieved.

Window Classes

One of the global variables, 'szWindowClass', contains the name of the class associated with your window. Every window has a class name associated with it. A window class is not the same as a C++ class, it is simply a structure that contains vital information about a window.

In the generated project, there is a function called 'MyRegisterClass' which populates a window class structure and calls 'RegisterClassEx' which is a Win32 function responsible for registering window classes with the system. Window classes must be unique.

The WNDCLASSEX structure is defined thus:

```
typedef struct _WNDCLASSEX {

        UINT cbSize;

        UINT style;

        WNDPROC lpfnWndProc;

        int cbClsExtra;

        int cbWndExtra;

        HANDLE hInstance;

        HICON hIcon;

        HCURSOR hCursor;

        HBRUSH hbrBackground;

        LPCTSTR lpszMenuName;

        LPCTSTR lpszClassName;

        HICON hIconSm;

    } WNDCLASSEX;
```

Any number of windows can be created using this class, but they will all have exactly the same properties and behaviour. Let's look at the elements of WNDCLASSEX.

The Elements of WNDCLASSEX

There are a number of elements to a window class, each dealing with a specific aspect of a window created with this class.

cbSize
The size of a WNDCLASSEX structure. This is used by Windows internally for version control. It should always be set to 'sizeof(WNDCLASSEX)'.

style
Specifies the class styles. It defines how the window should behave under certain circumstances. See the Visual C++ help for a detailed explanation of the various options.

lpfnWndProc
This is the address of a function that behaves as the window's message handler.

cbClsExtra
You can allocate extra memory to store class specific information if you wish. This member tells the system how much memory to allocate.

cbWndExtra
Extra memory can also be initialised for each window instance.

hInstance
A handle to the application instance that contains the message handler. This will nearly always be set to the current applications instance handle.

hIcon
A handle to the icon for this window class. Obtained by calling LoadIcon.

hCursor
A handle to the cursor that will be displayed when the mouse is over your application window. Obtained by calling LoadCursor.

hbrßackground

A handle to the brush which should be used to paint the background of your window.

lpszMenuName

The resource identifier of the menu to be used in your application window. Menus are created in the resource editor.

lpszClassName

The name you decide to give to your class. This name will be used as a unique identifier to create windows with this class.

hIconSm

A handle to a small icon to be associated with your window. If this handle is set to NULL, the hIcon member is searched for a 16x16 pixel icon.

Not all of these members have to be used, but if you decide not to use them you should set them to NULL to ensure that correct results are given.

There are already some pre-defined classes which are defined by Windows when it initialises. They are classes for commonly used windows like buttons, edit boxes, list boxes, etc, which save you having to develop your own controls.

This is also good for the user because as long as you use the pre-defined control classes, the user has a common interface between applications.

Once you have registered a window class, it remains registered for the lifetime of your program. You do not have to register it every time you want to create a window that uses it. In fact, if you do try and register the same class more than once, you will get an error telling you that the class already exists.

Now that you have registered a class, you will need to create a window that uses it.

Creating Windows

Look at the InitInstance function in your WinApp project. You will notice that it contains a call to the CreateWindow function. CreateWindow will create a window with the settings you specify and register it within the system, then it returns to you a handle to the window.

You will see various types of handles when programming in Windows. A handle is basically an identifier to an object within the Windows system. Handles are used to identify windows, files, memory, COM ports, bitmaps, icons, etc.

```
hWnd = CreateWindow(szWindowClass, szTitle,
            WS_OVERLAPPEDWINDOW,
            CW_USEDEFAULT, 0, CW_USEDEFAULT, 0,
            NULL, NULL, hInstance, NULL);
```

CreateWindow or CreateWindowEx are used to create any kind of window. The window class that was registered previously is one of the arguments to CreateWindow which specifies things like the icon and message handler for the window.

As mentioned, there are many pre-defined classes. These can also be used as an argument to CreateWindow to create standard controls.

Z-order of windows

The Z order is the order in which windows are displayed. When you create a new window it is placed at the top of the Z-order. When you activate a window it is moved to the top of the Z-order.

REMEMBER

The Z-order of windows can be changed at any time.

You can create windows with a special style that are 'topmost' windows which means that they always stay at the top of the Z-order.

Hierarchy of windows

The first window created by an application is generally known as the top-level window. Top-level windows do not have a parent.

...cont'd

Top-level windows are created relative to the top left corner of the screen. Child windows are created relative to the top left corner of their parent window.

One of the parameters to CreateWindow is a parent window handle which specifies the parent of the window you are creating. Windows that are created within windows are called *children* of the window in which they are created. Child windows also need to be created with a specific style.

Once a window is created it is not necessarily visible. Look at the code in InitInstance:

    ShowWindow(hWnd, nCmdShow);

    UpdateWindow(hWnd);

These two functions display and update the window.

hWnd
This is the handle of the window returned by CreateWindow.

nCmdShow
Specifies how to show the main window. This parameter is passed through from WinMain.

When you create a shortcut to a program in Windows, you can specify that the application be opened minimized or maximized. If you use the parameter specified in WinMain your application will behave as the user expects it to.

Look at the different windows types within Windows: edit boxes, list boxes, buttons, checkboxes, etc. They are all windows that are created using CreateWindow or CreateWindowEx but they all look and behave radically different because of the different styles that they are created with.

Messages, Queues and Loops

What are messages, and what are they used for?

Messages are Windows' way of communicating between applications and the system. Messages are sent *to* your application to notify you that certain operations have been performed. For example, the user changing the colour scheme of their PC.

HANDY TIP

To get an idea of the messages used in Windows, look at the Spy++ utility which is explained on pages 74–75.

Messages are also sent *by* your application to notify the system that your application has performed certain operations.

But most often, messages are sent between the Windows *in* your application to notify them that something must happen or that something has happened.

A message is nothing more than a data structure. It is a data structure that has six members:

```
typedef struct tagMSG {

        HWND hwnd;

        UINT message;

        WPARAM wParam;

        LPARAM lParam;

        DWORD time;

        POINT pt;

} MSG;
```

hwnd
This stores a handle to the window that the message is destined for.

message
The message identifier for this message. Each message has a unique identifier.

wParam
The first parameter to this message.

lParam

Another parameter for this message.

time

The time at which this message was posted in the queue.

pt

The screen position of the mouse cursor when the message was posted.

Remember that a Windows application is the same as any other in that once the entry-point has terminated, the application has finished its execution and is unloaded.

If you simply created a window and then exited your WinMain function your program would terminate and your window would be destroyed – not much use to anyone.

The Message Loop

How do we get around this problem? Well, at the end of WinMain you will notice these lines of code:

```
while (GetMessage(&msg, NULL, 0, 0))

{

        if (!TranslateAccelerator(msg.hwnd, hAccelTable,
&msg))

        {

                TranslateMessage(&msg);

                DispatchMessage(&msg);

        }

}
```

Does the while loop look familiar? Basically, this code is responsible for keeping your application alive. The 'GetMessage' API takes the message at the front of the message queue and stores it in the 'MSG' structure which is defined at the top of WinMain.

Once the message is received, the next step is to translate any accelerators. TranslateAccelerators takes any key commands and translates them into command messages for keyboard shortcuts. For example, it would translate the message for 'CTRL+V' into the 'Edit|Paste' command.

The message is then translated and dispatched to the message handler for the window that the message is destined for.

The Message Queue

The message queue is simply a data structure that holds a list of messages waiting to be processed. The message queue is a FIFO (First In First Out) queue which means that each message has to wait its turn to be processed. You cannot put a message at the front of the queue for faster processing.

You can put messages into a message queue in one of two ways. If you use 'SendMessage' the message is put in the queue, but SendMessage does not return until the message is processed. The return value of SendMessage is the return value of the message handler.

The other alternative is to use 'PostMessage'. PostMessage will put the message into the queue and return immediately.

To put a message into another windows message queue you do not need to declare and populate an entire message structure. The SendMessage and PostMessage functions just need the window handle, message code and the parameters to the message. The other members of the MSG structure are filled in for you.

Each message exists for a particular reason, and messages are used for all sorts of things in Windows. It is up to you to decide what your window will do in response to messages by handling them in your message handler.

Message Handlers

A message handler is also often called a window procedure.

A message handler is a function which messages are dispatched to. Remember that the message handler is a member of the WNDCLASSEX structure so there is one message handler for every class of window.

For example, all edit controls use the same message handler. This ensures that all edit boxes behave in the same way.

The message handler is called a 'callback' function because it is a function in *your* code which is called by the system when an event occurs.

The concept of an event-driven system takes some getting used to if you have always written sequential programs.

Windows programs are event driven which basically means that your program does not call a function that receives input from the user. Instead, when input is taken from the user, an event occurs and your window is notified of that event.

The prototype for a message handler is:

```
LRESULT CALLBACK WndProc(
    HWND hWnd,
    UINT uMsg,
    WPARAM wParam,
    LPARAM lParam);
```

You have probably noticed that the parameters to the message handler are the first four members of a MSG structure. It makes sense when you think that this is a message handler.

The parameter uMsg refers to a unique message ID that tells you what has happened or what should happen. There are literally hundreds of message identifiers so it seems ridiculous to expect you to handle all of them, right?

There is a default message handler that is built into Windows. Look at the message handler in WinApp on the following page:

WndProc itself is generally a very simple function. It usually contains a big switch statement that chooses what to do, depending on the message being handled.

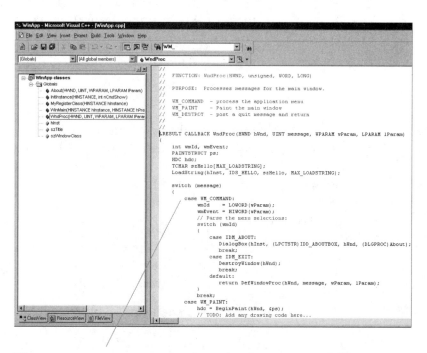

Command messages are sent to your window when menu items are selected, or buttons are clicked.

There are some messages that also have many different options for their parameters. For example, look at the WM_COMMAND case handler: it contains a second switch which splits the code up even more depending on which identifier the command message came from.

Look at the bottom of the message switch. There is a default case statement which captures any unmatched identifiers. Notice that, in this case, the parameters are passed straight to a function called DefWindowProc. This is the default window procedure (message handler).

Think of your message handler as a message interceptor. It gives you the ability to intercept a message and perform certain tasks based on that message. Then you can either pass the parameters (or modify them first) on to the default message handler or simply return.

Spying On Messages

As mentioned, there are literally hundreds of message identifiers within Windows. You can usually tell what a message is for by its identifier. For example, messages that are destined for an application window generally take the form of WM_xxxxx where WM stands for Window Message and the latter part is the message description itself.

Messages destined for controls have their own prefix. Listbox messages are prefixed with LBM, edit box messages are prefixed with EM and so on.

Messages that are sent back from controls are called notification messages because they notify their parent that something has happened. These have the M replaced with an N, so a combo box notification is prefixed with CBN. You get the idea.

There is a complete reference to all of the messages in the online help.

A very good way of looking into Windows and seeing what goes on 'under the covers' so to speak is to use the 'Spy++' utility. It is a very useful tool which spies on the messages being sent between windows.

You can launch Spy++ by select the Spy++ icon in the Visual C++ tools program group.

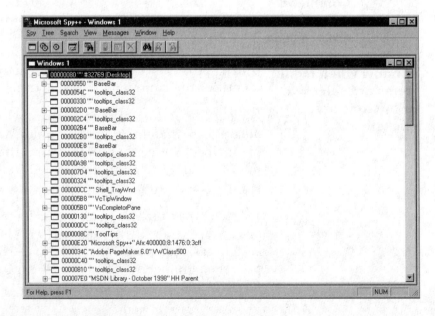

...cont'd

If you are learning to program for the Windows platform, then this is an invaluable tool.

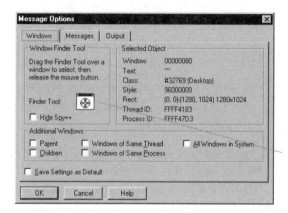

Select the 'Messages' option from the 'Spy' menu and you will be asked to choose which window you want to spy on. Use the finder tool to find a window to spy on by dragging it over a window.

Spying on windows is a good way of getting ideas about how to program things.

By using this tool you also have a good way of seeing how other Windows applications are structured by moving the window finder tool around your screen and seeing the different windows that make up the user interface of applications.

When you click OK, Spy++ will start spying on the window that you have selected. You can spy on more than one window at a time so you can see the interactions that occur between windows, for example when you drag and drop information between them.

Once spying, you may find that as you move your mouse over a window that you are spying on, too many messages are displayed. You can turn off individual messages or groups of messages by checking and unchecking the relevant boxes in the message options dialog box.

To stop spying on a window, simply click the icon in the toolbar.

Try spying on the window for WinApp and see just how many messages are used in Windows – you will be amazed!

Dialog Boxes

The kind of windows that we have been looking at so far are generally the main window of an application. In Visual C++, for example, the first window created is most probably the window in which all of the other windows are displayed or docked. This is the main application window of Visual C++.

Sometimes you may want to present the user with a temporary window that just pops up to collect some information from the user and then disappears again.

For this purpose you would use a dialog box. Now, do not think that dialog boxes are not windows, because they are. They are just a different kind of window.

In Visual C++ when you start to create a new project, you are presented with the following window:

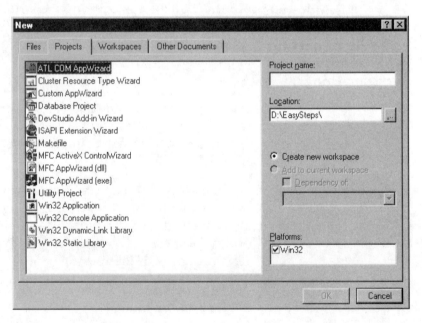

This is a dialog box. It contains controls which gather information and is only on the screen temporarily. It is not present for the entire time that you are in Visual C++.

In WinApp a dialog box is created for you. You can display it by selecting the 'Help|About' menu option.

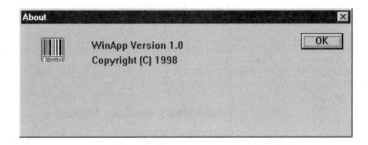

This is a fairly simple dialog box in comparison to those included in Visual C++ but it gives you an idea of how they are programmed.

The message handler for the main window handles the command message that is generated when you click the About menu option. The following function call is then made:

```
DialogBox(hInst,

        (LPCTSTR)IDD_ABOUTBOX,

        hWnd,

        (DLGPROC)About);
```

As you can probably guess, 'DialogBox' is a function responsible for initialising and displaying a dialog box.

A dialog box is created and displayed based on a dialog template resource in the module specified by hInst. Dialog box resources can be created in Visual C++. IDD_ABOUTBOX is the identifier of the dialog box in this case.

Dialog boxes must have a parent window which dictates where in the Z-order that the dialog box will appear.

The final parameter is the all important window procedure for this dialog box. Dialog boxes do differ from other windows in this respect because, although they all have the same class, each one can have a different message handler.

There are two different types of dialog boxes that you can use: 'modal' and 'modeless' dialog boxes.

Modal dialog boxes

Modal dialog boxes will capture the focus of an application and the application will not continue to execute until the dialog box has been terminated. WinApp's About dialog box is a modal dialog box.

Modeless dialog boxes

Modeless dialog boxes allow the application to continue running while they are displayed. They are still used as a temporary window but they can be used to log events or some other operation that cannot suspend the program.

Modeless dialog boxes are created in a slightly different way, using the function 'CreateDialog:'

```
HWND CreateDialog(HINSTANCE hInstance,

    LPCTSTR lpszTemplate,

    HWND hParent,

    DLGPROC lpfnDialogFunc);
```

You will notice that the parameters are exactly the same as those for DialogBox.

Message Boxes

There is another special kind of window: the message box. It is essentially a modal dialog box but you do not need to create a template for it.

The template for message boxes is created and displayed by the system. All you need to do is call a function, 'MessageBox' (as follows on the next page).

...cont'd

int MessageBox(HWND hwndOwner,

LPCTSTR lpszText,

LPCTSTR lpszCaption,

UINT uType);

hwndOwner
A handle to the window that will own the message box.

lpszText
The text that is displayed in the client area of a message box.

lpszCaption
The text that appears in the title area of the message box.

uType

HANDY TIP

Message boxes are a quick, easy way to prompt the user with information or questions.

The type of message box that is to be displayed. There are many different options that can be specified through the uType parameter.

The type of message box can affect which icon (if any) is displayed, which buttons are displayed, which is the default button and other system settings.

The return value of MessageBox can depend upon the type of message box you use. You can have a message box which has Yes and No buttons in which case, the return value of MessageBox would be IDYES or IDNO.

The return values are identifiers created with the '#define' macro to give meaningful names to the values.

Message boxes can be a good way of performing simple runtime debugging of your applications. For example, you may have a dialog box that isn't being displayed and you want to know if it is actually being created properly. You could put a call to MessageBox in the message handler to see if any messages are being sent to your dialog box.

Multiple Document Interface

Another kind of top-level window that you will see a lot is the Multiple Document Interface (MDI).

An MDI window allows the user of your application to have several documents open at the same time. The document editing area of Visual C++ has an MDI.

When an MDI window is created, it creates a client window in which the document windows are created. Each client window is known as an MDI child window and cannot move outside the bounds of the MDI client window.

The child windows can be tiled or cascaded within the MDI client area.

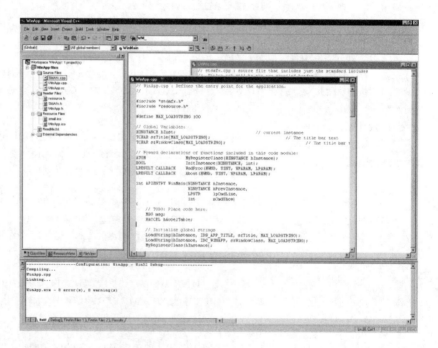

Now, you should have enough information to be able to create a Windows application yourself. Remember, you can use AppWizard to generate a lot of this code for you.

Try changing the handler for WM_PAINT to do something a little more adventurous!

Dynamic Link Libraries

There are more slight differences to take into account when developing Dynamic Link Libraries (DLLs). For instance, DLLs have a different entry point again:

```
BOOL WINAPI DllMain(

    HINSTANCE hinstDLL,

    DWORD fdwReason,

    LPVOID lpvReserved);
```

hinstDLL

The instance handle for your DLL. This should be used with functions that require a module handle.

fdwReason

The reason that your DLL has been loaded. Use this in your entry code to decide what actions to take.

lpReserved

This is a reserved parameter which is generally set to NULL.

The entry point of a DLL is called for different reasons but most often it is called when a process attaches to or detaches from your DLL.

In the early days of Windows, DLLs were a good way to promote the re-use of code. If you have a function that is used in many applications you can store it in a DLL. This way, the DLL only needs to be distributed once rather than distributing this code many times.

Also, if there is a bug in your function for some reason, you can fix the bug in the DLL and redistribute just that one DLL. You do not have to redistribute every application that uses it.

When you create a DLL an import library is also created which you link into other projects so that the compiler knows where to get all of its code from.

When you create an application that uses your DLL you have a choice as to how the two will be linked.

If you link the export library into your application the DLL that contains the code you are using will be loaded into memory at the same time as your application. You can call any functions directly. If the DLL cannot be found when you load the application, the application will not load.

Your other option is to load the DLL yourself at run time. If you do this, you cannot just call functions directly because the compiler did not store the addresses of the functions when you linked your application. You will have to get the address of the functions yourself.

To load a library you use the 'LoadLibrary' API and to get the address of a function, use the 'GetProcAddress'.

In order to make sure that functions in DLLs are available to other applications they must be *exported* from your DLL. There are two ways to export functions from your DLL: use a module definition file or use special compiler directives.

If you use a module definition file (.def extension) you must list the functions that you want to export in an EXPORTS section of the file.

Another way of exporting functions is to use a special compiler directive: _declspec(dllexport).

DLLs do have their drawbacks, however. Sometimes you get customised versions of DLLs which have the same name as others or just a later version of a DLL which has the same name. This DLL isn't necessarily compatible with all applications that use it, which makes it less easy to use.

Chapter Five

Resources

In this chapter you will learn what resources are and how to create and manipulate them.

Covers

What Are Resources?

Resources are basically binary data that are linked into your application when you create it. There are several different types of standard resource that are supported by Visual C++ but you can also create your own custom resources.

When an application (or DLL) is loaded its resource table is also loaded which contains all of the resources that are bound into the executable.

Resources are linked into your program so you do not need to distribute extra icon files or bitmaps.

Remember in WinApp where we populated the WNDCLASSEX structure? Look in the function MyRegisterClass. You will notice that two resources are loaded from the WinApp executable: IDI_WINAPP is loaded to provide the main icon for your window and IDI_SMALL is loaded to provide the small icon that is displayed in the top-left corner of your window.

There is also another resource loaded, but an instance handle of NULL is specified. That is because the cursor IDC_ARROW is loaded from the Windows system so no instance handle is needed. Resources obtained from the system are often called 'stock resources'.

Linking large bitmaps into your application will make it large and slow to load. Consider distributing the bitmaps separately.

You will notice that resources are loaded with a 'Load*Resource*' function where the name of the resource provides the second part of the function name. For example, to load icons you use LoadIcon, to load cursors you use LoadCursor.

As well as loading resources from your executable you can also load them from files on disk so you do not have to link them into your program.

Resources can be created within Visual C++ but do not have to be. In fact, there are many third-party commercial icon editors available for creating icons. You can use icons created elsewhere as a resource for your application.

You can view the resources that are linked to an executable by clicking on the ResourceView tab of the Workspace window:

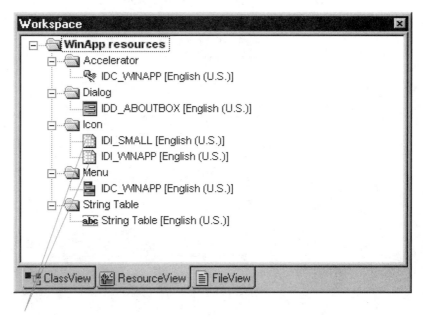

Here, you can see the two icons that were loaded in MyRegisterClass in the 'Icon' section.

When you built WinApp you may have realised that the first line of output in the Output window was a line that reads *"Compiling resources..."*. Again, you do not have to do anything yourself to compile and link the resources into your application. Visual C++ makes this all part of the build process.

If you want to add extra resources to an application you can click the right mouse button on 'WinApp resources' and select 'Insert...' from the menu.

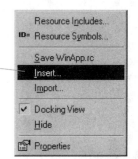

You will then be presented with the following dialog box (page 86) which allows you to choose which resource you want to insert.

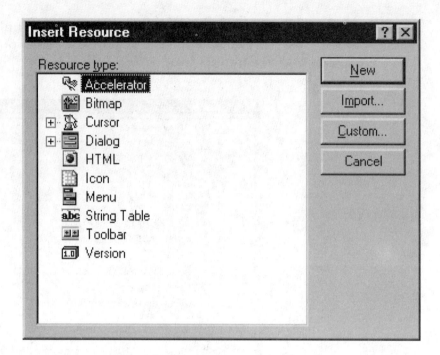

Choose the type of resource that you want to add and click
'New'.

As you can see there are ten supported resource types with
the facility to create custom resource types.

When you create custom resources you are presented with a
blank file in which you must enter your own binary data. So
this option is for the more advanced Windows programmer.

If you select the Import option, you can choose to import
icons, wave files, cursors, Visual Basic forms or HTML
files. The file that you import will then appear in
ResourceView.

Resources must be identified with a unique identifier
which can either be a numerical value or a literal string.
For example, your icon can be identified as IDI_ICON or
"IDI_ICON".

Resource Symbols

Resources generally have a symbol associated with them, a symbol that is defined with the #define macro. The symbol is simply a unique number that identifies the resource in question. The symbol is to give it a meaningful name.

If you click the right mouse button on WinApp resources in ResourceView you will see a menu item called Resource symbols.

Selecting this option will display the Resource Symbols dialog box:

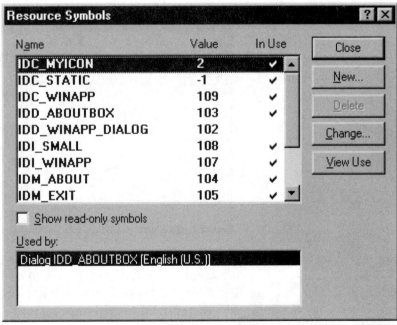

The Resource Symbols dialog shows you the symbols that are defined for the resources in your application and where they are used. You can also create new symbols here if you want to create new symbols but not necessarily attach them to an actual resource yet.

Now let's look at each of the different resource types that Visual C++ supports and see how to create and use each of them.

Accelerators

Accelerators provide you with a mechanism to associate keyboard shortcuts with specific actions. For example, the 'CTRL+C' shortcut is generally used to copy items to the clipboard.

An accelerator table is a collection of key accelerators. It simply associates a key combination with a command message. Look at WinApp's accelerators by double-clicking on 'IDC_WINAPP' in the 'Accelerator' section of ResourceView:

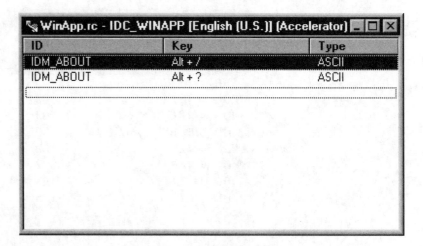

The 'Help|About' menu item has been associated with two key combinations: 'Alt+/' and 'Alt+?'. If you execute WinApp and try one of these key combinations you will see that the about box will appear.

If you want to add another accelerator, double-click on the empty entry at the bottom of the list. You will see the 'Accel Properties' dialog box:

REMEMBER

Keyboard accelerators are widely used and they are almost expected by users.

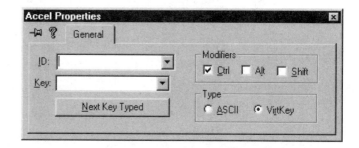

If you want to modify an existing accelerator you can double-click on it and the same dialog box will be displayed but will obviously be populated with the accelerator's properties.

Set the ID (the resource symbol) that you want this accelerator to be associated with. Whenever the user presses the key combination specified here a command message will be sent to your main window with the ID specified in this dialog.

You can select a virtual key such as the F-keys at the top of the keyboard or you can click on the Next Key Typed button which will record the next key pressed as the key accelerator.

If you want the user to have to hold down special keys like Shift, Ctrl or Alt then check the relevant boxes.

You can choose between ASCII or VirtKey code types but be careful when choosing because if you use ASCII characters they are not necessarily the same in all countries. This is only really a problem however if you plan to distribute your application worldwide.

Accelerators are a good thing to use, but try and make them correspond with other applications to give your user a common interface. For example, use 'CTRL+C' for copying items to the clipboard.

Bitmaps

For those of you who are not aware, bitmaps are basically pictures. A bitmap represents a rectangular area of the screen as wide and high as the bitmap. When a bitmap is displayed, it defines the colour of the area that it covers on the screen.

Bitmaps are stored in a file with the .bmp extension and can be read by most image editing packages.

There are no bitmaps in WinApp but you can add one easily by following the steps in the section 'What Are Resources?' (pages 84–86).

Insert a bitmap and Visual C++ will look like this:

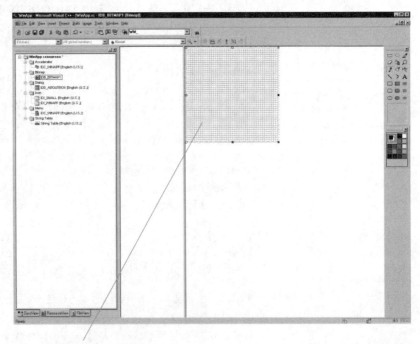

The bitmap has been created and is ready to be edited in the document editing area of Visual C++. The bitmap has been assigned the symbol IDB_BITMAP1 but that can be changed to suit your application.

Changing the properties

To change the properties of your bitmap select 'Properties...' from the 'View' menu (or press Alt+Enter):

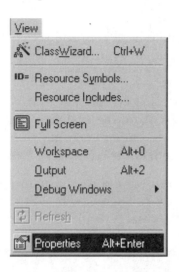

There is also a Properties option on the menu that appears when you right click on the resource symbol. This displays the properties of the bitmap resource rather than the properties of the bitmap itself. If you want to change the dimension or colour depth of the bitmap, select this option.

If you are viewing the properties of the bitmap itself you will see this dialog box:

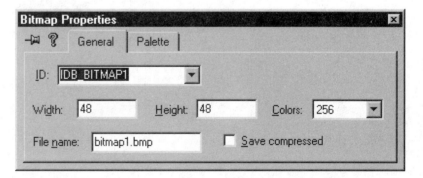

As you can see, this dialog box gives you the ability to change any details of the bitmap, including the palette colours.

Bitmaps can be loaded into your application by using the LoadBitmap function.

If you want to load a bitmap from a file, you can use the LoadImage function.

Cursors

Whether you realise it or not, you use cursors every time you use a mouse with your PC. A cursor is the picture that shows you where your mouse is pointing.

Generally your mouse cursor is an arrow but it changes depending on where your mouse is. For instance, when you move your mouse over the corner of a resizable window, it turns into a two-headed arrow.

In MyRegisterClass, you saw that WinApp loads the cursor IDC_ARROW from the system. There are many other system defined cursors as well. Just think about all the times that your mouse cursor changes its appearance.

HANDY TIP

Always try to make your cursors easy to see on any background.

WinApp doesn't contain any custom cursors so add one now, then you can see how to edit them. Visual C++ should now look like this:

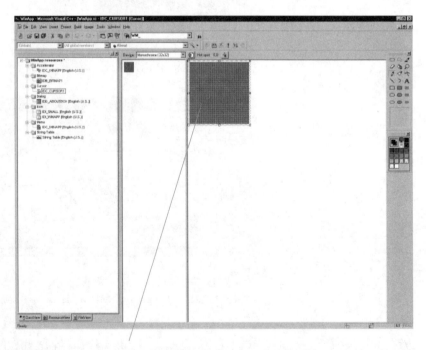

You are presented initially with what looks like a monochrome bitmap. Cursors are essentially bitmaps but they do have a couple of additional features.

...cont'd

For instance, they have two extra entries in their palette which bitmaps do not have: inverse and transparent.

Inverse

Any pixels set in your cursor with this entry will invert the screen pixel underneath it.

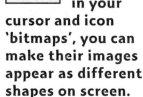

By making pixels transparent in your cursor and icon 'bitmaps', you can make their images appear as different shapes on screen.

Transparent

Pixels in your cursor that have the transparent attribute will not overwrite what is on the screen. This is why the arrow cursor is not rectangular, despite the fact that cursors are essentially bitmaps so they actually occupy a rectangular region.

Note the controls above the cursor editing area:

These tell you the kind of cursor that you are editing and where the hot spot of the cursor is. The hot spot is a single location within the cursor which is used as a reference for mouse operations such as button clicks.

You can edit the hot spot by clicking on this icon:

It's probably fair to say that you'll want more than two colours so you need to know how to add extra device images to increase the amount of available colours:

Click on this icon or press the Insert key. The New Cursor Image dialog box appears.

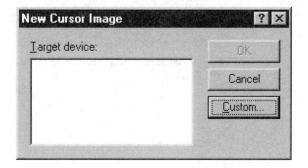

Click on Custom and then select the height, width and colour depth that you want to apply to your new cursor image from the Custom Image dialog box.

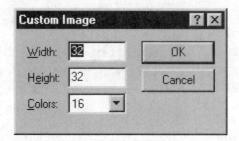

Every window has a cursor associated with it. Most application windows use IDC_ARROW but child windows and controls may use different ones. The edit control, for example, uses the text insertion cursor.

Every time the mouse moves inside your window a message is sent to your window procedure, WM_SETCURSOR, allowing you to change the cursor when the mouse moves over a certain point in your window if you wish.

Try creating your own cursor for WinApp, then change the function call in MyRegisterClass that loads the cursor so that it loads your cursor instead.

Dialog Boxes

We have already discussed the code involved in making a dialog appear. Now it's time to look at how a dialog box's layout is designed.

As mentioned before, the About box is a dialog box and if you look at ResourceView you will see that it has a resource ID of IDD_ABOUTBOX.

Double-click on IDD_ABOUTBOX and the dialog template will be loaded into the resource editor, allowing you to make changes.

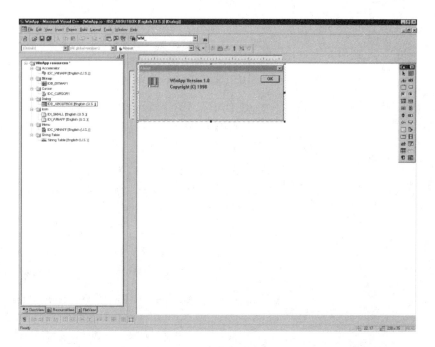

You can now edit the way that the About dialog box looks.

There are several controls that you can place in a dialog box and they can be seen in the Controls toolbar.

To add controls to the dialog template, simply drag and drop them from the Controls toolbar onto your dialog template. From there you will be able to move and resize them however you like.

If you want to change or view the properties of a control in a dialog template, click it once to select it and then press Alt+Enter or select Properties from the View menu.

To view the properties of the dialog box itself, click an area without a control and press Alt+Enter or select Properties from the View menu.

HANDY TIP

Change the font for the dialog box from System to MS Sans Serif. This will make it look more like a standard Windows application.

HTML Resources

With HTML resources you can integrate web pages into your application. There are functions within Windows that will handle the displaying of an HTML page for you by using Microsoft's internet browsing technology.

You could, for example have an HTML page as your about box and have a hyperlink within it to your email address so that people can get in touch with you about your product.

When you add an HTML resource to your project a new HTML document is created and displayed in the document editing area of Visual C++.

The document editor in Visual C++ recognises HTML as a document format so, like with your source code, recognised keywords will appear in a different colour.

In order to access HTML resources from your application, you can also load the resource into Internet Explorer by using the new protocol specifier, 'res'. Whereas with a web based URL you would prefix the URL with *http://*, if you are accessing a resource you prefix the application name with *res://*.

HTML is obviously far too large a topic to go into here so we will simply say here that it is possible to include HTML resources in your project.

Icons

Most people will know what icons are, not least because Windows is smothered with them. Icons were used primarily for launching applications but they are being used more and more in toolbars and Windows controls.

You can create icons in Visual C++ or you can import them from a file with the .ico extension. However, Visual C++ only supports icons with up to 256 colours so if you do want high colour icons you will need to create them in a third-party package.

You will notice that there are two icons in WinApp: IDI_WINAPP and IDI_SMALL.

Double-click on IDI_WINAPP and it will be brought into the Visual C++ resource editor.

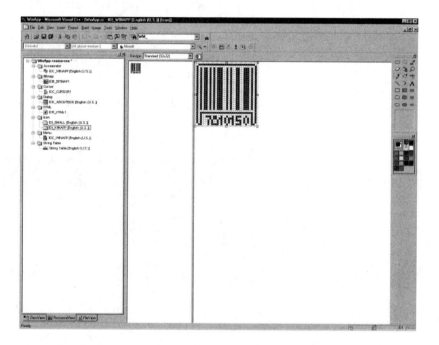

Editing icons is exactly the same as editing cursors except for one obvious difference: icons do not have hot spots, therefore no button is present for setting the hot spot.

Other than that, the toolbars are exactly the same and changing the properties is also identical.

An icon is not just used for the system menu of a window or to put in the about box. Icons are also used in list controls and tree controls. You can load and draw icons any time you like so you could have your own uses for icons.

Icons are loaded with the LoadIcon function and drawn with the DrawIcon function.

Menus

The most obvious use for a menu is in an application's main window. It sits at the top of the window under the title bar and contains options that perform specific actions.

Each item on a menu has a resource symbol associated with it which sends a command message to the window that owns the menu. Quite often, menu items will share that resource symbol with a key accelerator to perform the same action. For example, in WinApp, 'Ctrl+/' performs the same action as the 'Help|About' menu item.

Double-click on the IDC_WINAPP menu in ResourceView to see what the menu looks like when you are editing it:

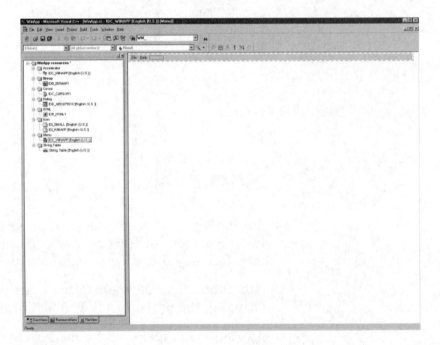

Visual C++ makes it easier to edit menus by displaying them in the editor in the same way that they appear in your window.

If you click on the File or Help menu item you will see the options under each of them.

...cont'd

As with creating new accelerators, to create a new menu item just double-click on the empty item and you will see the 'Menu Item Properties' dialog box.

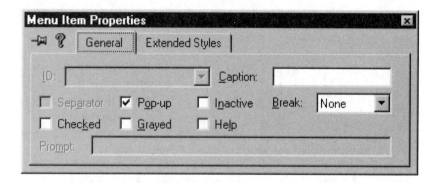

HANDY TIP

Try to make your menus as standard as possible. This makes the user instantly comfortable with your application.

If you are adding or editing lots of menu items you can keep the properties dialog box on the screen by clicking this icon: 📌

The ID that you assign to each menu item is a resource symbol which is kept in the list of resource symbols for your application.

Once you have created your menu and you want to assign accelerators to certain menu items you can select the identifiers from the list that has been created for you.

Menu items are generally displayed with a letter underlined so that you can use the keyboard to display the menu by holding down the Alt key and pressing the underlined letter key. To underline a letter in your menu name, prefix the letter with an ampersand (&) character.

This tells the resource compiler that you want the next letter underlined. To see an example of this, double-click on the File menu in IDC_WINAPP.

Menus can also be displayed when you click the right mouse button in a certain place. These are called popup menus or context menus.

String Tables

String tables are exactly what their name suggests they are. A string table is a list of strings each of which has an associated identifier.

The strings are loaded from the table by using the LoadString function which, using the identifier, locates the string and returns it to you.

String tables are used primarily for localising applications. You can have a string table relating to each language that you will have your application translated into. That way, you don't have to search through all of your code finding and replacing strings.

Because you use a numerical identifier to locate the strings it doesn't matter what language the application is running in until the actual string itself is being used.

String tables are also a convenient place to store regularly used strings such as the name of your application. If you store the application name in the string table and you decide to change it at a future date, you only need to change it once, in the string table. Otherwise, you have to go through all of your code looking for strings that contain your application name.

For an example of string tables in action, look at the top of the WinMain function in WinApp. There, the application name and window class name are loaded from the string table using the LoadString function.

Toolbars

Toolbars are another way of quickly sending commands to a window. A toolbar is a collection of buttons, each of which has a bitmap which is displayed on it and an associated resource symbol which specifies the command that it sends to its owner window.

When you edit a toolbar in Visual C++ you are presented with the same editor as with bitmaps which makes sense seeing as each toolbar button is basically a bitmap.

 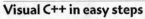

Add a toolbar to WinApp and you will see that, in a similar way to editing menus, a representation of what your toolbar will look like is shown in the editing window.

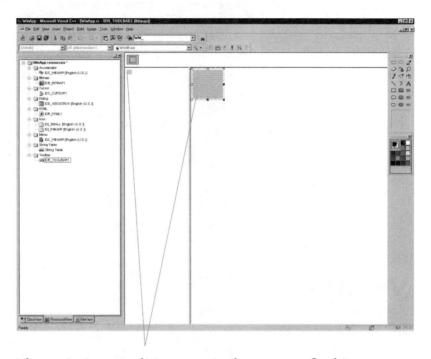

The main image editing area is the same as for bitmaps, cursors and icons. There is a smaller pane to the left which shows an actual size picture of the button bitmap that you are editing.

The pane above the editing area shows the toolbar as it will look when loaded into your window.

You can change the properties of a button in one of three ways: double-click on the button in the pane that represents the finished toolbar, press 'Alt+Enter' or select the 'Properties' entry from the 'View' menu.

As with accelerators, each toolbar button can be associated with an existing resource symbol for a menu item which will result in the relevant command message being sent to the window when the toolbar button is clicked.

To change the properties of a toolbar button, modify the settings in the 'Toolbar Button Properties' dialog box.

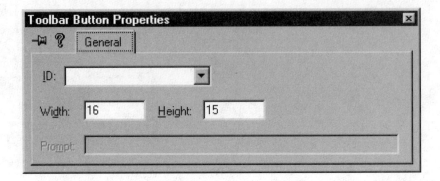

It is possible to vary the height and width of toolbar buttons but it makes sense to keep them all at least the same height, if not the same width as well.

Version

Version information is very important if you are to keep track of where you are at with your application. The version resource contains various pieces of information relating to your application.

To change the information in this structure:

1 Select the item that you want to change.

2 Click it again to edit the contents.

Remember to update the version information whenever you release an update to your application. If you do not update version numbers there will be great confusion when you are trying to track down problems in the future.

Programming With Class

Chapter Six

In this chapter you will learn how easy object oriented development is with classes. We will also look at the functionality provided by the Microsoft Foundation Classes (MFCs).

Covers

What Are The MFCs?

Microsoft Foundation Classes (MFCs) make application development much easier and faster for you.

With MFCs you are also provided with a complex framework on which to build your applications. You can then extend or override parts of the framework to create your own applications. The framework does a lot of the work for you when it comes to window handling, file handling, etc.

As you may have guessed by the name, the MFCs are a collection of C++ classes which cover most aspects of C++ programming, especially for Windows.

 In your Visual C++ box you get a chart which shows the hierarchy of the MFCs.

Nearly, but not all of the foundation classes are derived from the 'CObject' base class. The CObject class itself is not of much use but it does provide some useful diagnostics code which you can use in your CObject derived classes.

When you create an MFC based project the AppWizards have a lot more options for you to choose from when creating your project files, which demonstrates the extra functionality that is provided by MFCs.

When you install Visual C++ you have an option to install the source code for the MFC. This is a good idea if you want to actually see how the MFCs and the framework are created.

You should not think of MFC based applications as *different* to Win32 applications. They are Win32 applications which support the use of MFCs. Underneath all of the C++ wrappers you essentially have a Win32 application.

Messages are handled in a slightly different way with MFC windows. The framework provides a message handler which handles many messages for you. However, because the MFC framework is made up of C++ classes, you reap the benefits that C++ brings over C such as inheritance, polymorphism, overridable functions, etc.

Although an MFC window will handle a lot of the messages for you, it does not do so exclusively. You can override the message handler functions in your own derived class, thus providing your own implementation of a message handler.

When overriding base class functionality, you still have the functionality of the base class available to you. You can call the base class implementation of the function that you are overriding before or after your code, or not at all. This means that you can extend the functionality provided by the framework rather than replacing it and having to rewrite a lot of code.

There is no limit to the levels of inheritance. This means that you can have as many levels of functionality as you like extending the functionality all the time. Look, for example at the CTreeView class – it has about five levels of derivation.

In the C++ help pages, you are told which functions are overridable in a class so you get a good idea of the functionality that you are able to extend or replace.

The MFCs are being extended all the time to include support for the new Windows common controls and other aspects of Windows programming.

Another good thing about inheriting implementation from base classes is that you can create new controls very easily. For example, if you want to create a new tree control, you can use the structure of the existing CTreeCtrl class and just override aspects of it in order to create your own tree control.

There are far too many classes to discuss in any detail in this chapter but it will give you an overall view of the classes used in application creation and window management. For all the utility classes you will have to refer to the Visual C++ documentation.

Some More About Classes

In chapter three we looked briefly at what classes are and how to declare them but you really need to know in more detail how classes work and how to use them.

In the last few pages also there have been a few new words which you will see a lot of when programming with classes. If you are going to succeed in the world of object oriented programming you should really understand the meanings of words like polymorphism and inheritance.

Inheritance

When you base a class on another class, you are said to be 'deriving' one class from the other. The derived class inherits the functionality and attributes of the class that it is based upon. The class that the functionality is inherited from is called the 'base class' of the 'derived class'.

For example, you may have a base class called 'CInsect'. However, you decide to be more specific and declare a number of classes that demonstrate the behaviour of different insects, such as the ant, fly, etc.

You would have a class called 'CFly' which is derived from the 'CInsect' class. CFly would have all the same attributes as CInsect such as legs and body, but you can then extend it by adding fly-specific elements such as wings.

Polymorphism

Polymorphism is when you have two classes, the member functions of which behave differently but have the same definition.

Normally, to call the member functions of a class you need to tell the compiler what type of object you are using so that it can verify the existence of those functions.

However, thanks to *late binding*, Visual C++ does not need to know the type of the object at compile time because it does not bind the function names to the objects until run time.

For example, take the following code:

```
CAnimal *pAnimal;

CDog *pDog = pAnimal;

pAnimal->Speak();

pDog->Speak();
```

REMEMBER

The functions don't necessarily have to be different.

Suppose that two classes have been defined: 'CAnimal' and 'CDog'. 'pAnimal' is a pointer to a class of type 'CAnimal' and 'pDog' is a pointer to a class of type 'CDog'. Both classes implement a function called 'Speak' which have different code in them.

Notice that pDog is made equal to pAnimal so that they both point at the same memory location.

When you use pAnimal to call Speak, the CAnimal implementation of the function is called.

When you use pDog to call Speak, the CDog implementation of the function is called.

What happens at run time is that the type of the pointer is checked to see which implementation of the function to call rather than this being done at compile time.

Many people make the mistake of thinking that in order to use polymorphism, one class must be derived from another but this is not necessarily the case.

When you think about windows, and all the different types of windows, you will realise the power that you gain by using inheritance and polymorphism and the more you program under Windows with MFCs, the more this will become apparent.

The best thing to do now is to create a project that uses the MFCs. Then we can add some of our own classes as well as instances of some of the MFCs. Then we will look at how to use ClassView, ClassWizard and the WizardBar.

Creating MFC Projects

When you create a new project, you are presented with three project types that support the use of MFCs. Start creating a new project and you will see these options around the middle of the list.

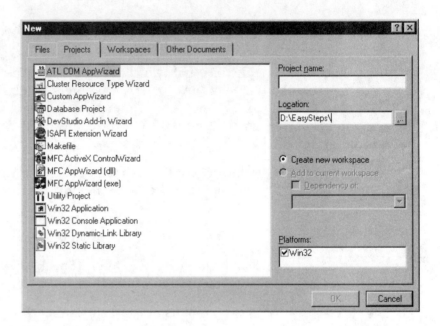

There are three project types that use MFCs: ActiveX controls, DLLs or applications. Each project type creates very different source files and output which perform specific tasks.

We have already discussed the different project types and what they are used for. The first MFC project we are going to create is a simple MFC application so that we can look at using classes without getting bogged down with lots of other details.

Create an MFC application by following these steps:

1 Select the 'MFC AppWizard (exe)' project type.

2 Type the name 'MFCApp' and click 'OK' to start the AppWizard.

...cont'd

3 Click on the 'Dialog based' application type and click 'Next'.

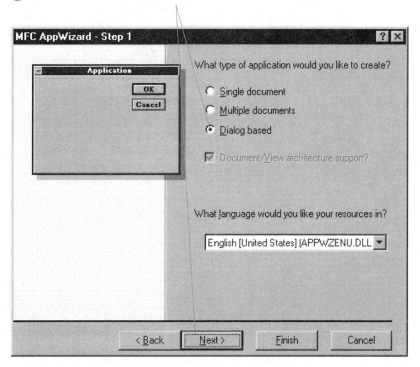

Leave all of the other settings as default to finish the creation of your project.

When the project is created, Visual C++ will load the dialog template into the resource editor. This dialog is the main window of your application.

Dialog based applications are very quick and easy to make. You can apply certain styles to the dialog box to make it look like an application window too by giving it a system menu, minimize button and maximise button.

Now you have a template application which supports the use of the MFCs. Let's look at adding a new class and how to manipulate that class using ClassWizard, ClassView and WizardBar.

ClassView

When we created a Win32 application project there were no classes in ClassView, only global functions. Well, now you can see ClassView in all of its glory:

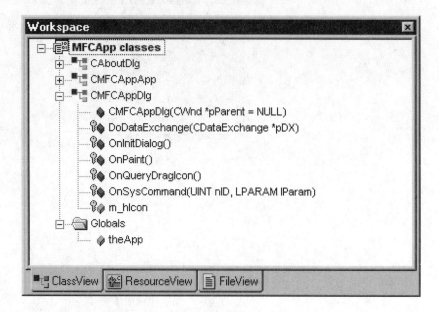

Each of the elements of ClassView are designated with different icons:

▪️🔩	Classes
♦	Member functions
🔑♦	Protected member functions
🔒♦	Private member functions
◆	Data members
🔑◆	Protected data members
🔒◆	Private data members
▦	Projects

Adding a New Class

The AppWizard does generate some classes for your application but at some point you are going to want to add more classes to add functionality to your application.

As with most things in Visual C++ there are a few different ways of adding a class to your project:

HANDY TIP

Classes are a very good way of storing and protecting data.

To add a class to your project, click the right mouse button on the project name in ClassView and select New Class from the menu.

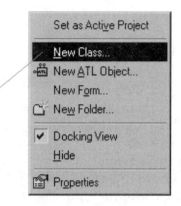

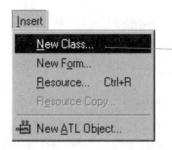

Or you can select the 'New Class' option from the 'Insert' menu.

Alternatively, if you have the WizardBar toolbar displayed you can select New Class from the WizardBar actions menu.

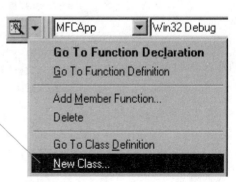

You will then be presented with the 'New Class' dialog box.

REMEMBER

To access classes' variables or functions from anywhere in your application, include the header file in 'stdafx.h'.

When adding a new class to your project you have three options: an 'MFC Class', a 'Generic Class' or a 'Form Class'.

MFC Class

Selecting this type of class will add a class to your project that is derived from one of the foundation classes.

Generic Class

With this option you can add your own classes to your project. This class does not need to be derived from a foundation class.

Form Class

A class which is based upon a dialog template resource. This will create a class derived from form classes such as CDialog. If the document/view architecture is included, the new class could also be derived from CFormView.

Create a new class which is a generic class called 'CInsect'. You can change the names of the source files that are generated for your class if you wish, but the defaults are generally acceptable.

Your new class will now appear in ClassView. A default constructor and destructor are also created for your class.

It is not a required convention, but it is general practice to prefix classes with a capital 'C' to denote that it is a class. Visual C++ caters for this when creating the source files for your new class.

The files are named after your class but without the leading 'C'.

If you are going to access this class from other source files you must remember to include the header file for your class in the relevant source code files.

Adding Member Variables

In order to add data members to a class in your project, right click on the class name and select the 'Add Member Variable...' option.

You will then be prompted for information regarding the new member variable.

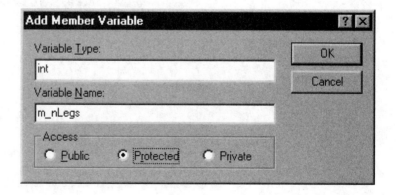

The fields are as follows:

Variable Type
The type of this new variable. It can be any of the built in data types or one of your own types defined with the 'typedef' keyword.

Variable Name

The usual convention for naming member variables is to prefix the variable name and type with "m_".

Access

Choose whether this variable is to be public, protected or private. This will dictate the access that other functions and classes will have to this variable.

You will notice that, with the new dynamic ClassView, your new member variable appears immediately.

Adding Member Functions

To add a function to a class, right-click on the class name and select 'Add Member Function...' from the menu. You will then see a dialog box similar to the Add Member Variable dialog box.

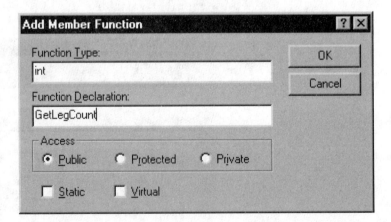

Complete the dialog and click OK to add the new member function.

Function Type

The return type of this function can be any variable type.

Function Declaration

The name of the new function.

 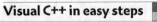

Access

The same as with member variables. This dictates the access that other classes and functions will have to this function.

Static

Static functions are members of a class that can be called without having an instance of the class. Therefore, static members should not rely on member variables because they will not exist if the function is called without instantiating a class first.

Virtual

A virtual function is one which you expect to be redefined in derived classes. The function only needs to be defined as virtual in the base class. In derived classes it is automatically assumed to be virtual.

Again, the new function is displayed in ClassView immediately. You are then taken to the line in the source code file that defines the function ready for you to start adding code to the function body.

Navigating With WizardßBar

Visual C++ makes it easy to find functions within your code. You can use ClassView to navigate to functions by double-clicking on their names. However, you do have to expand the relevant levels of the tree in ClassView to do this.

The WizardBar makes it easier to navigate through code by giving you combo boxes from which you can choose the class name (or globals) and member function that you wish to view/edit.

Class   Filter   Members

As soon as you select a class and a member you are taken straight to the line of code that defines the function in question.

MFC ClassWizard

We have looked at ways of adding data members and member functions to classes. This is a general method for any classes in your project, MFC or otherwise. When it comes to manipulating MFC based classes there is another, more specific tool: 'ClassWizard'.

The MFC ClassWizard will handle any classes in your project that are derived from one of the foundation classes. There are five tabs in the ClassWizard, each of which provides you with different operations to perform on your classes:

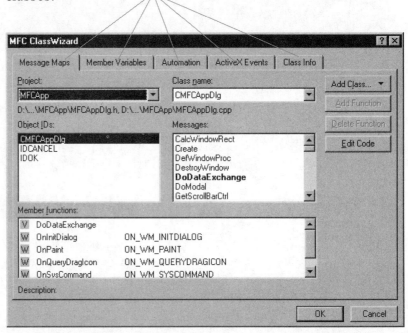

REMEMBER

The CInsect class will not appear because it is not a class based on a foundation class.

Message Maps

ClassWizard makes it easier for you to add support for handling messages to your application. It helps you to add support for notification messages that are sent by child windows as well as adding support for messages that are sent to your window by the Windows system.

...cont'd

As you select the different items in the *Object IDs* list, the messages that relate to that object are displayed in the *Messages* list. When you select the class itself (at the top of the list) all messages relating to that type of class are displayed.

Member Variables

Obtaining information from dialog controls is not a particularly difficult task but it is time consuming if you have a large number of controls in your dialog box. It can also make code look messy.

The MFC framework has a mechanism called *dialog data exchange* (DDX) which is a mechanism for exchanging data between dialog controls and the dialog class's member variables.

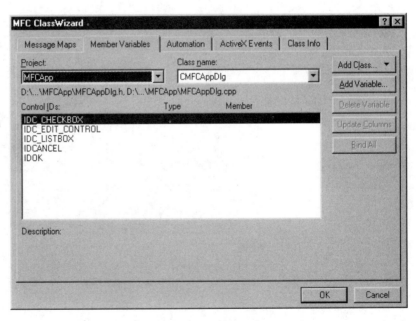

BEWARE
Some extra controls have been added to the MFCApp dialog template to demonstrate this feature, so your ClassWizard will not be identical to this.

When you enter the Member Variables tab you will be presented with a list of the identifiers in the dialog box template.

You can change the class being displayed and even the project (if you have more than one project in your workspace) by selecting one from the drop down list boxes labelled *Project* and *Class name*.

You can then associate a member variable with a dialog identifier.

1 Select the ID that you wish to associate a variable with.

2 Click the 'Add Variable' button.

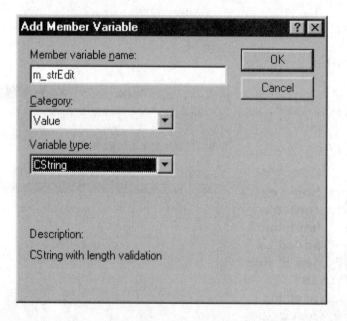

The member variables that are associated with the dialog controls can either be associated with the control itself or the data contained within the control. For example, if you were to choose an edit control, you could associate a member string variable (a CString class) with the text contained within the edit control or you could associate an edit control member variable with the edit control itself.

The controls are derived from the CWnd class which provides the functionality of a window. Therefore, associating variables with the control itself gives you access to the window functionality of that control so that you can pass messages to the control using its own member functions.

With some controls you can use different member variables to represent the data in the control. For example, the edit control can be associated with a CString class to contain the text in the control but it can also be associated with a LONG or an int data type if the edit control is to store a numerical value.

ActiveX and Automation
These tabs are specific to ActiveX controls or projects that support automation. These will be looked at in the next chapter.

Class Info
This tab just gives you information about the classes in your project, like the files that implement the class, the base class and any associated resource IDs for dialog boxes.

Message Maps

Depending on how you look at it, message handling may or may not be made easier with MFCs.

If you are used to programming using the Win32 SDK you are probably happier with a message handler like the ones we looked at in chapter four where you just have one function and a big switch statement.

Otherwise, you are probably used to the VB approach where you associate a function (or subroutine) with a particular event.

In an MFC project you can use message maps. Message maps are a way of mapping messages to functions. A message map is basically a collection of macros that associate a message or a notification with a member function of the class.

When you click the 'Add Function' button, ClassWizard will generate an entry in the message for the class in question and create a member function of the class so that all you have to do is add the function body.

Just to see how much easier message maps make it to handle messages, consider the code in WinApp that displays the message box. Within the message handler, there is a switch statement that chooses a path of code depending on which message is sent to the window. Then within the WM_COMMAND handler, another switch statement checks which identifier sends the command. In an MFC application, this would be replaced by the following code in the message map:

```
ON_COMMAND(IDC_ABOUT, OnAbout)
```

. . . and you don't even have to add that yourself, because ClassWizard will do it for you with a few mouse clicks!

Frame Windows

The main window in an MFC application is called a 'frame window'. It is called this because it is a window which looks like a frame for your application.

If you decide to include toolbars and a status bar in your application, they are loaded into the frame so that the client area of the window is not affected by their presence.

In the case of a multiple document application, you have multiple frame windows. The main application window which contains the client area is one frame, and each of the child windows within the MDI client is also a frame window. Frame windows are generally used to contain a view (or multiple views) of a document.

Documents and Views

We have looked at Windows applications and we have looked at applications that use dialog boxes as their main window.

Another approach that applications use is to implement the document/view architecture. The document/view architecture is a 'document-centric' way of developing applications. Rather than being a different way of coding the same thing, the document/view architecture is a different way of looking at how data is stored and displayed.

If you have a set of information that you want the user to be able to view in different formats, the data is stored in a *document* and different *views* are associated with the document. For example, you may want to view a directory listing in a chart, or a simple list. The directory listing itself would be stored in a document, and the chart and list would be different views of that document.

This offers you the ability to quickly change the way that data is represented visually. Imagine if you had one window that displayed the chart or the list. It would need a flag to state which of the views was current and then two lots of drawing code, one of which would be implemented depending on the view being used.

Now take this to extremes and imagine having a hundred different views of the same data. The drawing code for your single window would be a nightmare! At least with individual views, each contained within its own class, you would have self-contained views of the data. Also, because of the benefits of C++ you could base views on other similar views which would minimise the amount of code that you would have to rewrite.

Not surprisingly, MFC has support for the document/view architecture. CDocument is the class that supports the document itself and CView (and various derivatives) support views of the document.

Another advantage of the document/view architecture is apparent when it comes to serialisation (ie, loading documents from and saving documents to a persistent medium such as a disk file). All of the data is in one place – the document class – making serialisation so much easier.

When you created 'MFCApp', remember that we selected the dialog based project type. There were also two other options: single document and multiple document.

Single document

The single document application is an application which has support for one document (hence the name) and has a window that is similar to Notepad or Wordpad – a single document interface with one view of the document.

Multiple document

A multiple document application still only supports one document and view type by default but implements a multiple document interface so that more than one document can be edited at any one time.

When you create an MFC application, you can choose whether to implement the document/view architecture or not. If you do not implement the document/view architecture the major difference is that you do not have the document class. The main frame window is still created and a view is still created but it has no document associated with it.

If you choose to implement the document/view architecture, the application registers a document template which includes a file extension and description of the type of document that your application will manipulate.

ActiveX

In this chapter you will learn about the latest programming craze: Componentware. You will also learn how to develop and use ActiveX controls.

Chapter Seven

Covers

What is ActiveX?

It all started with a technology called Object Linking and Embedding (OLE). It was originally introduced so that users could embed objects from one application into another. For example, you have been able to link an Excel spreadsheet into a Word document for some time now.

As is always the case, this technology evolved, and Microsoft decided that the technology had to become more flexible. When OLE version two arrived, Microsoft realised that it provided more than just compound document support but it provided a mechanism for applications to interact in a more advanced way.

They soon realised that this new technology could be used for a lot more than just embedding documents into other documents, and started to develop applications that used OLE, not just to embed documents, but to embed controls, etc.

As OLE was historically associated with compound document support, Microsoft decided in 1996 to substitute the name OLE for a new name, ActiveX. This was at a time when ActiveX was being heavily integrated with Internet technologies.

Microsoft's Internet Explorer has added support for running ActiveX controls from within web pages, Visual C++ had added support for embedding ActiveX controls into dialog boxes. Suddenly ActiveX was becoming very popular.

In the past, for two applications to have any sort of interprocess communication, you would have to invent some sort of protocol for those applications to talk to each other. This would usually involve defining your own message identifiers and flinging messages back and forth between your applications.

In order to introduce a standard way that applications could communicate with each other, Microsoft introduced a technology called the Component Object Model (COM).

COM, as you may guess by the name, is a model for building component based software.

The idea behind COM is twofold. Firstly, components implement *interfaces* which are a way of using services in other components. Secondly, it encourages the re-use of existing code because applications can be broken down into smaller components which export their interfaces so that other applications can use them.

COM is now being very widely used by Microsoft. Nearly (if not all) of their applications are component based. The operating systems that they develop are very much 'componentised' with the Windows shell providing many services through COM interfaces.

Applications that support ActiveX and ActiveX controls themselves are built upon COM to ensure that these standard methods of communication are used.

ActiveX controls are stored within a DLL which is a regular Win32 DLL. There are some extra exports in the DLL however that allow the ActiveX controls to register themselves with the system.

Applications that support ActiveX controls are called ActiveX containers. The main shell of most Microsoft applications is an ActiveX container and many of the toolbars, etc, are loaded into it as ActiveX controls.

Internet Explorer is probably the best example of an ActiveX container. Word documents can be loaded in Internet Explorer and it will then take on the appearance of Microsoft Word with Word's menus and toolbars appearing in the user interface of IE.

As usual, the best way of understanding something is to have a practical example, so let's create an ActiveX control!

Creating an ActiveX Control

Create a new project, select the 'MFC ActiveX ControlWizard' project type and call the project 'AXCtrl'.

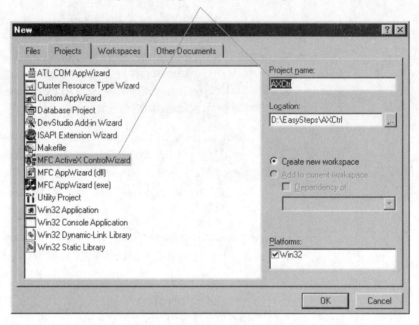

As with the other project types you will then be taken through the creation of the project step by step, choosing which options you wish to apply to your project.

For this project we are going to change some of the default options for the project, so we will step through the wizard for an ActiveX project.

The first step sets some general options for the project which you can leave as the default options.

We only want one ActiveX control in this project.

Do not have runtime licensing, this will just add unnecessary complication at this time.

Request source file comments, this will give you a better idea of what is happening.

Do not have help files to start with. These can be added at a later date and will just confuse things for now.

Click Next, and you should see the second step of the ActiveX ControlWizard.

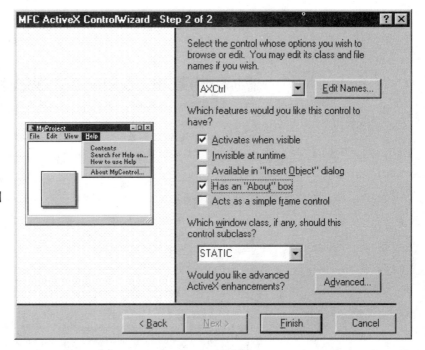

ActiveX controls can transform a web page by adding programmed functionality.

Do not change the name of the control at this point. You can do so if you wish but the rest of this chapter assumes that your control will be called 'AXCtrl'.

Change the options in this dialog so that they represent the dialog shown above. Our ActiveX control is going to subclass the STATIC window class. The STATIC window class is a window class that is registered by the Windows system, and it is used for displaying text, bitmaps and icons. Nearly all dialog control labels use the STATIC window class.

Enable the About box for your control. The About box is displayed when the AboutBox method is called in your ActiveX control. Methods are the names of functions that are exported via a COM interface. This will give you an example of what they look like without you having to do anything.

Click Finish to create the project and all associated files. You now have a project that includes a single ActiveX control.

Look at ClassWizard for your new project. You will notice a new icon.

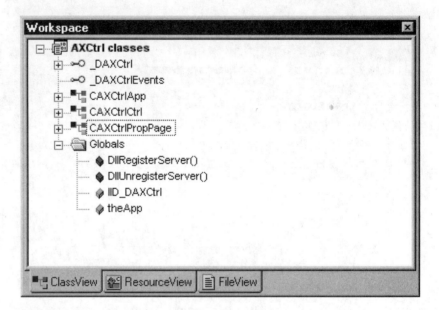

∞ This icon is used to represent an interface. An interface is essentially a class (redefined using typedef) with very specific member functions to ensure that it conforms to the COM.

In fact, there are some other new elements to this project. You will notice there are two global functions that are created for your project.

DllRegisterServer
This function is called when your ActiveX control is to be registered with Windows. It creates various Registry values which notify other applications of its existence.

DllUnregisterServer
The opposite of DllRegisterServer. This function will remove any Registry values relating to your project.

 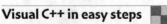

Notice that these functions refer to a server. Do not be fooled, this does not relate to a physical server. Remember, in the first ControlWizard step you were asked how many controls your project should contain.

HANDY TIP

Using DCOM you can access remote component servers.

Therefore, any global functions in your project cannot be specific to one control. Instead, your project is referred to as a server because, like a file server offers file services, your project offers ActiveX services.

Historically, OLE controls were stored in a file with the extension .OCX. (OCX incidentally stands for OLE control extension). An OCX file is just a DLL with a different filename extension, so it can still be treated like any other DLL and any DLL related API's can be used with it.

To register a server within Windows there is a utility called 'REGSVR32'. When you run this utility, it loads the server in question and calls the 'DllRegisterServer' function. If you pass the /u command line switch to REGSVR32 it will unregister a server, calling the 'DLLUnregisterServer' API.

When you build your ActiveX project, Visual C++ adds a custom built step to the project which will register your server. This simply calls REGSVR32 for you so that you do not then have to register the server yourself.

Your Control's Anatomy

Before we look at the ActiveX control itself in more detail, it is important to state that this chapter only offers a very high level view of COM and the interfaces that this project implements. Visual C++ makes it very easy to create ActiveX controls without you having to know about COM in great detail. COM is such a vast subject that it couldn't possibly be covered in this small chapter.

On the following page we will begin to look at the other elements of ClassView for AXCtrl.

_DAXCtrl

This is the dispatch interface for your ActiveX control. By using IDispatch, your ActiveX control will be available to more than just other C++ programs. Anything that supports using method names, such as VB and scripting, will be able to access your ActiveX control by using the method names.

Each method in an IDispatch interface is given a name. Similar to how message identifiers are mapped to a function in MFC message maps, method names are mapped to a function in dispatch maps.

_DAXCtrlEvents

In an ActiveX control, methods are a way that the container can tell the control what to do. However, sometimes it is necessary for the control to notify the container that something has happened.

This is where events come into play. Think about an edit control in a dialog box. To instruct the edit box to perform an action (like selecting some text) the dialog box would send a message to the edit control such as EM_SETSEL. If the edit control wants to notify the dialog box that an *event* has occurred it would send a message to the dialog box such as EN_CHANGE.

With ActiveX, the messages are replaced by methods and the events are replaced by events.

CAXCtrlApp

The main application class for this module is derived from the COleControlModule, which is in turn derived from the CWinApp class. This proves that this is a regular DLL but with some extra functionality for supporting ActiveX.

CAXCtrlCtrl

This is the class which contains the actual functionality of your ActiveX control. The functions that are mapped to methods in the dispatch map are members of this class. Notice the AboutBox function.

CAXCtrlPropPage

This class is responsible for the functionality of the property page for your ActiveX control. Once your control has been loaded into a container, you probably want to offer the user some way of changing certain properties of your control.

Adding Methods

It is probably quite likely that you will want more methods in your ActiveX control than just AboutBox. To add more methods to your ActiveX control, you can either:

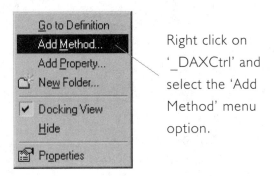

Right click on '_DAXCtrl' and select the 'Add Method' menu option.

Click the 'Add Method' button on the 'Automation' tab of 'MFC ClassWizard'.

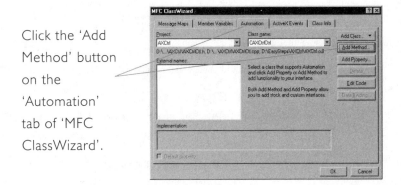

Whichever method you choose, you will be presented with the Add Method dialog box.

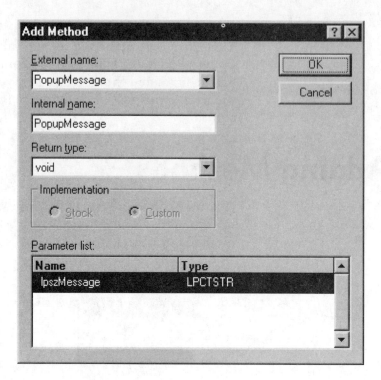

External name
You can choose one of the stock methods from the list or you can type in your own method name. We are going to add a method called PopupMessage.

Internal name
This is the name that is used by the control internally. By default, Visual C++ makes this the same as the external name, but you can change it if you wish.

Return type
The return type for this method. Exactly the same as return types for functions.

Implementation
If you choose a stock method from the list, you can choose whether to implement the stock method or to provide your own custom implementation of the method.

Parameter list

Edit the list of parameters to this method. Click on the list under the name heading and an edit control will appear into which you type the names of the parameters. Select the data type of the parameter as well.

For this example, the PopupMessage method will have one parameter: the message to display.

PopupMessage is a method which will simply display a message box with the text that is passed to it.

Adding Properties

Properties are exactly what the name suggests they might be – properties of the ActiveX control. Properties can be things such as a window caption, or the number of entries in a list. As methods are similar in purpose to C++ class member functions, properties are similar to C++ class data members.

Adding a property is the same as adding a method except that instead of choosing 'Add Method', you choose 'Add Property'. So, if you use the context menu of ClassView, select Add Property; or, if you use ClassWizard, select the Add Property button on the Automation tab.

You have three options when adding a property to an ActiveX control. You can either add a stock property, add a custom property as a member variable or add a custom property with get/set members.

Stock properties

There are a number of stock properties that are supported by Visual C++ which makes it easier for you to implement most commonly used properties. For instance, 'Caption' is a stock property. Most windows have a caption so it makes sense to support it.

Custom property as member variable

If you add a property as a member variable, you are enabling direct access to the member variable itself when reading or changing the variable. You have the option of adding a notification function that will be called when the property has been changed.

Custom property with get/set members

Sometimes you may want to add a property to an ActiveX control which cannot necessarily be represented by a static member variable – for example, it may be a property which has to be read from a database.

With this option, two methods will be added to your ActiveX control. One method will *get* the property and the other one will *set* the property. If your property is to be read only, you can eliminate the set property method which will remove the ability to set the property.

For AXCtrl, we will add a property called 'Number' which has get/set members.

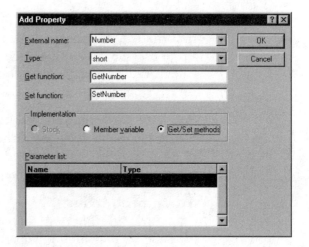

You will notice that Visual C++ does not actually add two methods to your dispatch interface, only the one property. There are, however, two`` new member functions in the cla s that is associated with this control. Also, a new entry h s been added to the dispatch ma

Adding Events

It is highly likely that, at some point in its existence, the ActiveX control is going to want to notify the container that something has happened to it. This is done by firing events at the container.

As with properties and methods, there are some stock events that are handled by the MFC framework and you can also add your own custom events.

To add an event you can either:

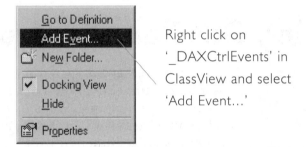

Right click on '_DAXCtrlEvents' in ClassView and select 'Add Event...'

Or click the 'Add Event...' button in the 'ActiveX Events' tab in MFC ClassWizard.

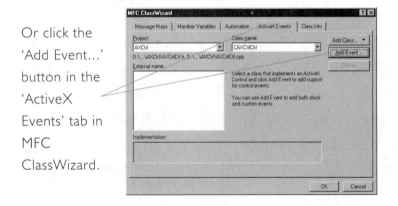

You will then be presented with the Add Event dialog box which prompts you for the settings for this new event.

This is a similar process to adding a property or a method. If you are adding a custom event, you must supply the name of the event. If you are adding a stock event, select it from the drop down list. If you choose a stock event from the list, the internal name is set to FireXxxx depending on the event that you choose.

If you decide to add a custom event, you must specify an internal name for the event, and if you wish you can add extra parameters to the event in order to supply extra information.

For AXCtrl, let's add the custom event, 'Click'.

An entry is added to the event map. Because it is a stock event it is not mapped to a member function in your class: it is handled by the framework.

Bulking Out Your Control

Now that we have prepared the ActiveX control, let's add some functionality to the PopupMessage method. Double-click on the 'PopupMessage' function in the 'CAXCtrlCtrl' class in 'ClassView'. In the code window you will see the PopupMessage function with a commented line which reads "// TODO: Add your dispatch handler code here".

Delete this line if you wish. It has no useful purpose other than telling you where to add your code.

In this function we are simply going to add a call to the MessageBox API. Add this line of code to the function:

```
MessageBox(lpszMessage, "AXCtrl Message", MB_OK);
```

This will display a message box which contains the text that is passed to the method. Note that *lpszMessage* is a parameter to this function.

That's all the code that we will add for now, but try adding more methods and different types of properties and experimenting with what works best for you.

There are some good samples that come with Visual C++ which demonstrate how to use ActiveX controls. Look at POLYCTL.

Testing Your Control

Now you should be able to build and test your ActiveX control. Press F7 or select Build from the Build menu to build your ActiveX control, the same as you would with any project.

The files in your project will be compiled and linked. If the build is successful, Visual C++ will then execute REGSVR32 in order to register your ActiveX control.

You should now be able to test your control. But as it is a DLL, so you cannot just execute it directly, how do you test it?

There is a tool that comes with Visual C++ called the 'ActiveX Control Test Container'. This is a very handy tool when it comes to developing ActiveX controls. It acts as a container for ActiveX controls, and allows you to call methods from within the controls so that you can test it without having to write your own ActiveX container.

Press Ctrl+F5 or select Execute from the Build menu to execute your ActiveX control. Visual C++ knows that this is not an executable application so it prompts you with this dialog box:

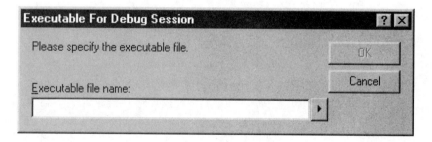

Click on the ▶ button and select 'ActiveX Control Test Container' from the menu. Click OK and the test container will be launched.

When the test container loads it will not insert your control straight away. You will have to do that manually.

Select Insert New Control from the Edit menu and you will see the standard ActiveX control selection box.

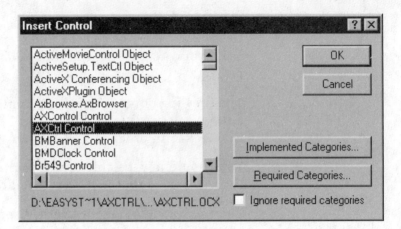

Select AXCtrl from the list and click OK. This will insert your new ActiveX control into the test container which should now look something like this.

To check if the events are working OK, do something to trigger the event. For example, in AXCtrl we added the stock Click event. So, if you click on your control you should see the following text appear in the bottom pane of the test container:

    AXCtrl Control: Click

This confirms that the click event has been fired.

If you want to invoke methods of an ActiveX control, select 'Invoke Methods...' from the 'Control' menu. You will then be prompted with a dialog box where you can choose which method to invoke and what parameters to pass to it.

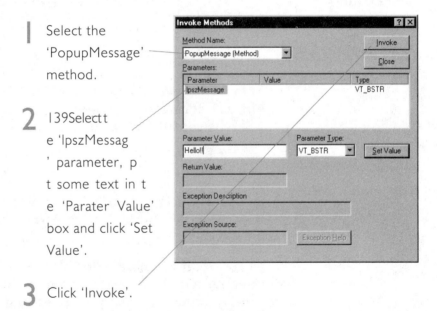

| Select the 'PopupMessage' method.

2 I39Select t e 'IpszMessag ' parameter, p t some text in t e 'Parater Value' box and click 'Set Value'.

3 Click 'Invoke'.

You should then see a message appear with the text that you entered as the parameter value.

There is also much, much more that you can do with the 'ActiveX Control Test Container'. For example, you can write your own macros so that you can automate the testing of your ActiveX controls.

Embedding Your Control in HTML

Suppose you have developed an ActiveX control that you wish to embed in a web page. You need to include the ActiveX control in your HTML code in an OBJECT tag.

The OBJECT tag should look something like this:

```
<object id="AXCtrl" name="AXCtrl"

classid="clsid:BD784085-8B68-11D2-B882-
0020182B6AB8" border="0"

width="131" height="62">

</object>
```

HANDY TIP **Try to keep your control small if it is going to be downloaded by people with slow modem links.**

Note that the clsid will be different for your control. To find the clsid for your ActiveX control, find the line that begins with:

```
IMPLEMENT_OLECREATE_EX(CAXCtrlCtrl
```

The line below will contain the clsid, but it will be in a different format than it needs to be in an OBJECT tag. It will look something like this in Visual C++:

```
0xbd784085, 0x8b68, 0x11d2, 0xb8, 0x82, 0, 0x20,
0x18, 0x2b, 0x6a, 0xb8
```

So you will need to rearrange the parts of the GUID so that they are in the correct format: xxxxxxxx-xxxx-xxxx-xxxx-xxxxxxxxxxxx.

Of course, if you have an HTML editor such as FrontPage then this will do the work for you. Simply add an ActiveX control to the page that you are editing and select AXCtrl from the list of ActiveX controls.

Property Pages

If you embed your ActiveX control into a web page or a dialog box, you will probably want to set the properties of the ActiveX control at design time rather than setting them dynamically when the control is actually running.

This is where the property page is useful. The property page is displayed whenever the properties of an ActiveX control are requested.

If you click the right mouse button on a dialog control and select 'Properties...' from the menu, this will invoke the property page of that control. It is the same for ActiveX controls.

Property pages are based on dialog boxes, and when they are displayed they display a dialog resource template. If you look at the resources for AXCtrl you will see a dialog resource called IDD_PROPPAGE_AXCTRL. This is the dialog resource for your property page.

Initially, your property page looks like this:

TODO: Place controls to manipulate properties of AXCtrl Control on this dialog.

Delete the TODO statement and add controls to the dialog template as you would do normally.

In order to associate the dialog controls with the properties of your ActiveX control you need to add member variables to the property page class 'CAXCtrlPropPage'.

Adding member variables to the property page class is the same as adding member variables to an MFC dialog (after all CPropertyPage is derived from CDialog).

However, there is one addition when adding member variables to a property page because you have to tell Visual C++ which ActiveX property the control is associated with.

Invoke the Add Member Variable dialog box by holding down the Ctrl key while double-clicking on a dialog control.

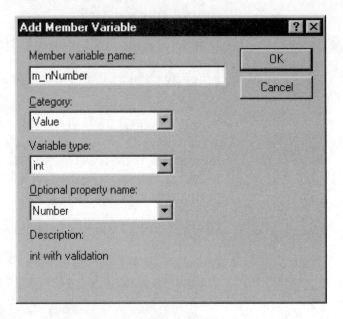

In the Add Member Variable dialog box, you can either select a stock property that you want the controls value to be associated with or you can type in the name of one of your custom properties.

The MFC framework adds entries to the relevent maps in order to establish the link between the dialog control and the ActiveX property.

Now, when you embed your control into a dialog box or another application, you will be able to view the properties of the control at design time and set the values of properties before they are actually executed.

Debugging

In this chapter you will learn how to load an application into the debugger so that you can watch variables and debug your application.

Chapter Eight

Covers

Debugging

So far we have built and executed all sorts of programs, but we have made one very heavy assumption: that your program will work first time.

This is all very well for the small, one-liners we have dealt with so far but when you start to develop more complicated programs it is inevitable that something is going to go wrong. For any of you that have done any programming before, you will know that this is the case.

It would be nice to think that we could always get it right first time but as this is not the case debugging has become a very important part of the development process.

Visual C++ makes debugging very easy for you by integrating the debugger into the same environment as your editor, compiler and linker. This means that you can edit, compile, link and debug applications, all without having to switch between different applications.

With the Visual C++ debugger you can perform many operations which make debugging your applications very easy. You can step into functions or over functions, you can run through code line by line watching variables as you go to see how they are affected by certain code. You can insert breakpoints in your code so that as soon as a particular line of code is about to be executed the debugger will be invoked.

A very useful feature of the Visual C++ debugger is the ability to *edit and continue*. Ordinarily, while debugging code, if you were to change the code you would have to rebuild your application and start debugging all over again. With edit and continue you can edit your code and when you continue stepping through your code, the single modified source file is recompiled and the program can continue running.

The rest of this chapter will look at how to use the debugging features of Visual C++ using the MFCApp project from chapter six.

Breakpoints

With breakpoints you are able to stop the execution of your program at any line of your code. Before you start debugging your application you need to tell Visual C++ where to stop executing your program so that you can get in there and find out what is going wrong.

Find the place in your source code where you want to put the breakpoint by using any of the methods we have looked at before and then insert a breakpoint. You can use any of the following methods to insert a breakpoint.

Press 'F9'.

Click on the 'Insert/Remove Breakpoint' icon 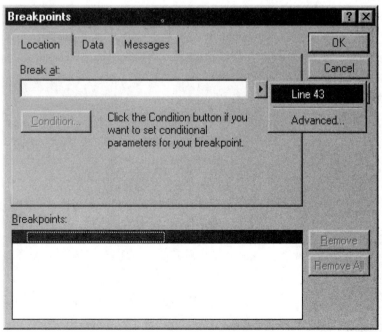 on the 'Build' toolbar.

Select 'Breakpoints...' from the 'Edit' menu (or press 'ALT+F9').

If you use the latter option, you will see the 'Breakpoints' dialog box.

With this dialog box you can view the current breakpoints, set the properties of breakpoints and add breakpoints.

Click on the ▶ button and then select 'Line xx' from the menu.

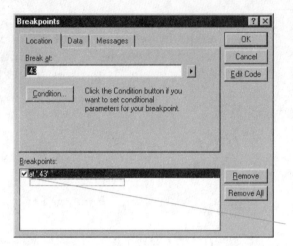

The breakpoint will then appear in the check list at the bottom of the dialog.

You can enable or disable the breakpoint by checking or clearing the boxes by the breakpoints.

Remove breakpoints by clicking the 'Remove' button, or all of them by clicking 'Remove All'.

You can create very advanced breakpoints by specifying that they are only active if a certain condition is met. The condition is the same as that used in an 'if' statement.

When a breakpoint is set, a red circle ● (trust me, it's red) appears in the selection bar next to your line of code. If you want to remove the breakpoint easily, you can just press 'F9' while the cursor is on this line.

You will notice that there are two other tabs in the 'Breakpoints' dialog box. These allow you to set breakpoints when certain messages are sent to your application or when the value of certain variables changes.

Once you have told Visual C++ where to relinquish execution of your program, you need to invoke the debugger.

Starting the Debugger

In order to start debugging an application, the project must be loaded into Visual C++. Load the MFCApp project from chapter six.

The debugger will be invoked when it encounters a breakpoint in your code or when an exception occurs, such as accessing an invalid memory address.

We will invoke the debugger manually by adding a breakpoint to MFCApp.

1 Load 'MFCApp.cpp' into the editor.

2 Go to line '43', which should be the start of the InitInstance function. Do this by selecting 'Go To' from the 'Edit' menu or by simply using the cursor keys.

HANDY TIP

F9 toggles breakpoints so pressing it again will remove the breakpoint.

3 Insert a breakpoint by pressing 'F9'.

You should now notice a red circle in the selection margin on the left hand side of the editor window. This denotes that a breakpoint has been set at that particular line of code.

Now, if you start this application in the debugger, it will stop just as it enters the 'InitInstance' function.

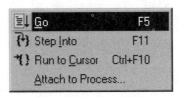

To start the debugger, select the 'Build' menu, then the 'Start Debug' submenu, and then select 'Go'. Alternatively, press 'F5'.

The Workspace window will then disappear as the debugger launches. You will also notice that some additional windows appear. These windows are obviously specific to the debugger which is why they are not normally visible.

The debugger should encounter the breakpoint and halt the execution of your application.

There is now a yellow arrow sitting on top of your
breakpoint. The line of code that the yellow arrow points to
is the next line of code to be executed.

Visual C++ will now look something like this:

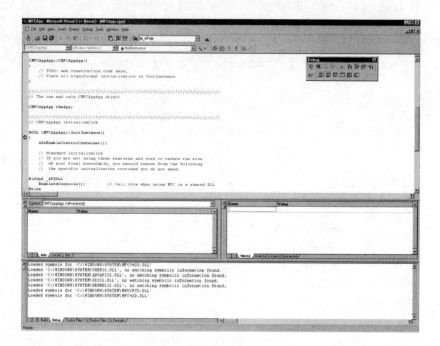

Your application is still loaded into memory, it is just in a
state of 'suspended animation' at this time. The debugger
itself is now activated so that you can view the contents of
memory, or look at the values of variables.

At this point you can either step through your code line by
line, continue running unrestricted or execute your code up
to the current cursor point. You are in total control.

Debug Windows

There are many other windows available to you while you are in the debugger which offer you more information about the state of your program.

While you have a program in the debugger, the 'Debug Windows...' submenu of the 'View' menu becomes active.

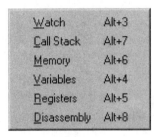

Each item on this menu displays a different debug window which can be docked the same as the watch window.

The Watch and the Variables windows are usually displayed by default (see screenshot opposite).

To view any of the other windows just select the relevant item from the menu or use the hotkeys.

Watch
This window allows you to watch variables as your code executes. As you step through your code, the variables will be updated automatically.

Call Stack
Displays the chain of function class that leads up to the point that you are currently debugging. Double click on any of the entries in this window to view the code in that function.

Memory
Displays the contents of memory. You can enter a variable name or an actual address to view the contents of memory at that point.

Variables
This window has three options: Auto, Locals and this. Using this window you can view the variables local to the function that you are debugging, the local variables or the members of the current class. This window also has a drop down list which displays the call stack.

Registers

You can view the contents of your PC's registers in this window. This is only really useful if you are comfortable with assembly level programming.

Disassembly

When you select this option the current source code is replaced by a view of the assembly code that your code is compiled into. Again, this is only useful if you are comfortable dealing at this level.

Watching Variables

One of the most common causes of problems in programming is with variables – eg, variables are being used in the wrong way or pointers are pointing in the wrong place.

That is why it is so important to know how to manipulate variables within the debugger. There are many ways to see what is happening with variables, depending on exactly what it is you want to see.

If you just want to see what happens generally to a variable you can use the Watch window:

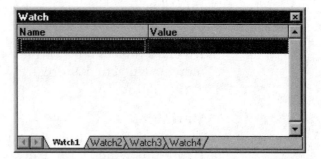

To 'watch' a variable, click on an entry in the watch window and type the name of the variable that you want to watch. Alternatively, you can drag the variable onto this window from your source code.

You can change the way that variables are represented in the Watch window by adding a suffix to the variable name. Here are a few examples of how to modify the view of a value.

variable,d	signed decimal
variable,x	hexadecimal
variable,f	floating point
variable,s	string

For a full list of the variable types see the Visual C++ documentation.

If you want to look at how the contents of a structure change you can use the Memory window.

This will show you the contents of memory starting at a given address. You can type in a memory address or the name of a variable in the Address box.

These windows are all well and good for viewing any variables, but if you want to view all of the variables in the local function, you don't want to have to keep dragging and dropping variables all over the place – or even worse, having to type them all in.

If you are jumping around from function to function whilst debugging, the Variables window really comes into its own.

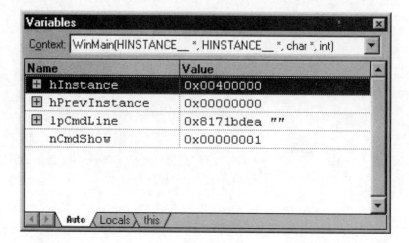

As you move from function to function, the variables that are local to each function are displayed in this window. This window also contains the call stack so that you can trace the path of execution which your application has taken.

Path of Execution

Even though your program runs line by line you do not necessarily have to watch it run line by line whilst you are using the debugger. The Visual C++ debugger has many features that allow you to change the way you run your program.

To continue executing your program from a breakpoint, click the ▤ button or press F5. The debugger will then continue to execute your program until it ends, another breakpoint is reached or the program finished.

If you want to step through your code, there are four options. If you are about to execute a function for which you have the source code available, you can step *into* the function rather than just executing it and seeing the result. Click the {} button or press 'F11'.

You can only step into functions that you have the source code for.

If you want to step over a function rather than executing every line of it, click the ⟨⟩ button or press 'F10'.

If you have stepped into a function accidentally, or you just want to step back out of it again you can do so by clicking the ⟨⟩ button or pressing 'SHIFT+F11'.

You may have the cursor positioned at a certain point in the source code where you think there may be a problem. You can tell the debugger to run your program until it gets to the line that the cursor is on by clicking the ⟨⟩ button or by pressing 'CTRL+F10'.

You can restart your application within the debugger by clicking on the ⟨⟩ button or by pressing 'CTRL+SHIFT+F5'.

Other Methods of Debugging

In order to debug programs with Visual C++ they do not necessarily have to have been launched from within Visual C++.

You can ask the Visual C++ debugger to attach to an external process by selecting the 'Build' menu, then the 'Start Debug' submenu and then selecting the 'Attach to Process...' item. Visual C++ will then display a list of running processes. You can then choose one to attach to and all of its modules will be loaded into Visual C++.

This process can then be broken into by selecting the Break option from the debug menu or by clicking the break button ⟨⟩.

Remember that if you do break into a program that you do not have the source code for, you will be presented with the assembly code rather than C code.

You can stop debugging any process by clicking the ⟨⟩ button or by pressing 'SHIFT+F5'.

Debugging as a result of a failure

If a debugger is registered with Windows (which Visual
C++ does for you) and a program crashes as a result of a
page fault or some such error, you will see a dialog box that
looks something like this:

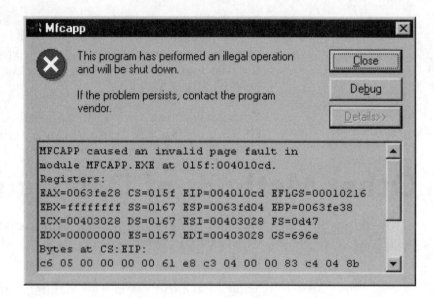

Don't worry, this was meant to happen! Now, if you click
on the 'Debug' button, the Visual C++ debugger will attach
itself to the process that has crashed and start debugging it
for you.

If this is an application for which you have the source code,
you will be able to see the exact line of code which has
failed.

If you do not have the source code available you will be
presented with the disassembly for the application.

Visual C++ Tools

In this chapter you will learn about the tools that come with Visual C++. Also, you will learn how to add your own tools to the Tools menu.

Covers

Chapter Nine

Visual C++ Tools

With Visual C++ you get many tools which are designed to aid you in your programming efforts. Some of them are very specialised and are designed with the more advanced programmer in mind, but most are general purpose tools.

The majority of the tools are accessible through the 'Microsoft Visual C++ Tools' program group which can be launched simply by clicking on them.

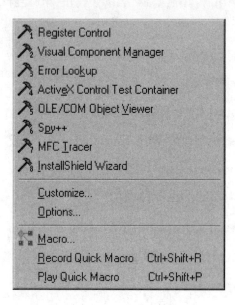

Some of the tools in the program group are featured on the 'Tools' menu within Visual C++.

A couple of the tools that are on this menu are not actually available through the program group such as the 'Visual Component Manager' and so must be launched from Visual C++.

The tools that appear on this menu are obviously those tools that you are most likely to need while you are actually working on a project within Visual C++.

Some of the tools such as the 'Register Control' option are actually command line utilities that Visual C++ passes parameters to.

Visual C++ gives you the facility to add tools to this menu, remove them or configure how they are used.

Customising the Tools Menu

To customise the tools, select the 'Customize' option from the 'Tools' menu. You will see the Visual C++ customisation dialog box within which you can customise many aspects of Visual C++.

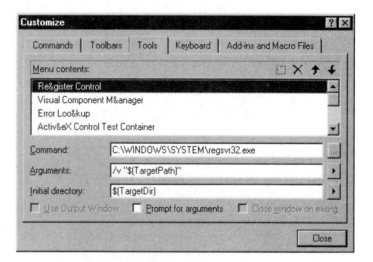

In order to configure the tools in Visual C++ click on the Tools tab and you will see the above dialog box. For each tool you can configure the command line, command line arguments and the starting directory.

To add a new tool to the menu, click on the ![button] button or click on the empty entry at the bottom of the list twice. You will then be able to specify the options for your new tool.

You can remove tools from the menu by clicking on the ![X button] button or selecting one and pressing the delete key. Be careful when removing tools though, because you cannot get them back easily.

If you want to change the order in which the tools appear, select a tool in the list and use the ![up] and the ![down] buttons to change its order in the list.

When you are customising a tool, you have several built in variables that you can use as program arguments or as a working directory.

Click on the  button next to the edit control for the program arguments or the working directory to see the list of variables that can be used:

Variables which can be used
as program arguments.

Variables which can be used
as program arguments.

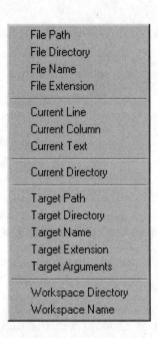

There are also three check boxes at the bottom of the Tools tab. If the tool is a console application it can use the Output window to display the results of running the tool.

If you want to execute the tool with different arguments, you can ask Visual C++ to prompt you for the arguments when you actually run the tool, rather than making them static.

Error Lookup

We have already looked at a couple of the tools that come with Visual C++ such as Spy++ and the ActiveX test container.

These tools did fit in very well with the chapters in which they were looked at. However, there are some general purpose tools which are worth a look at.

A very useful tool is the 'Error Lookup' utility. There is nothing worse than trawling through help files or, even worse, include files trying to find out what an error code means.

BEWARE **Pressing Escape will close the Error Lookup dialog box but it does not terminate the application.**

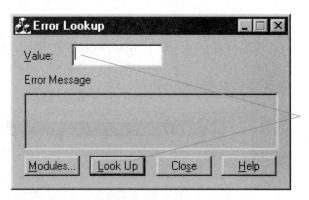

To find out what an error code means, simply type the error code in the 'Value' edit control and click the 'Look Up' button.

'Error Lookup' will then scan through some system modules to attempt to find an error message that relates to the code that you have supplied.

It may be that your error value is in a different module to those in the default list. If this is the case, you can click on the 'Modules' button to add more modules to the search list.

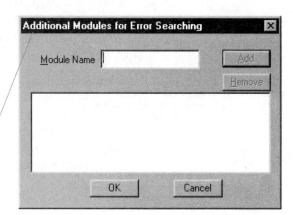

MFC Tracer

The MFC Tracer utility allows you to change the tracing options for the Microsoft Foundation Classes.

There are various TRACE macros that you can use in your code. When your project is loaded into the debugger the output of the TRACE macros is displayed in the Output debugger window.

The MFC framework also outputs information for you so that you can get real-time information about what is going on as your application executes.

By using this utility you can switch on and off the tracing of certain events.

To execute the utility, select it from the Tools menu in Visual C++ or from the icon in the Visual C++ Tool program group.

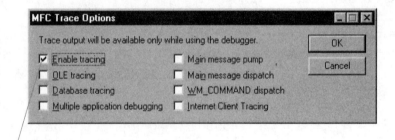

The most important checkbox is obviously the 'Enable tracing' checkbox. If this checkbox is clear, no tracing will be enabled irrespective of which other checkboxes are checked.

Check the items that you wish to enable tracing for and click OK.

If you want to find out whether tracing is enabled and which tracing options are enabled, you can do so by accessing the 'afxTraceEnabled' and 'afxTraceFlags' global variables.

Visual Component Manager

This utility helps you to achieve better re-use of code and better code sharing between teams. It is essentially a database of components.

REMEMBER

The Visual Component Manager is a very good way of promoting code re-use.

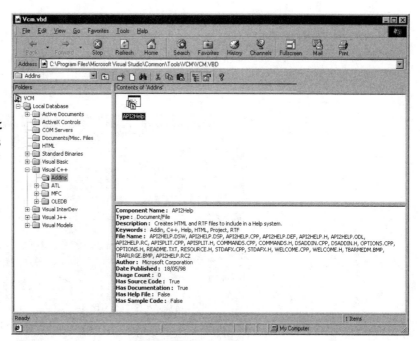

All of the components within the component manager are stored in a database. There are many items already in the database which are provided as sample components.

The database can be stored locally on your machine or it can be stored on a network drive allowing a whole development team access to each other's components.

The database is structured into folders so that you can easily find components in the future. You can create new folders if you want to include your own categories of components.

Any kind of component can be stored in the database whether it is an entire ActiveX control project or just a useful snippet of HTML code.

InstallShield Wizard

A cut down version of InstallShield is shipped with Visual C++. This version has limited functionality compared to the retail product but has enough functionality for you to be able to distribute the applications that you develop.

This version of InstallShield is also tied into Visual C++ to make it easier to use. When you select the 'InstallShield Wizard' from the 'Tools' menu you are presented with a wizard which gathers information about your project.

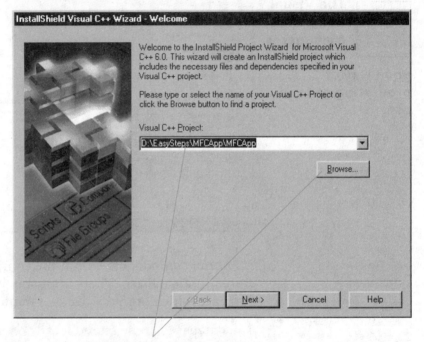

Choose a project that you want to distribute from the recent workspaces list or click Browse in order to browse for a project.

Then, supply some information about your application, and some information about your company.

Finally, the InstallWizard scans your application for any dependencies on shared DLLs and it adds them to the list of files that need to be distributed.

Then, when you click Finish, InstallShield will be launched with all of the information that you have supplied. You can then tailor your installation to suit your needs, changing the file groups if you want to include more files.

You can then create a setup package which will distribute your application.

InstallShield has been developed in close cooperation with Microsoft so you will reap some very important benefits from using InstallShield.

The installation of your application will comply with the Microsoft logo requirements. This means that your application will be registered properly and will have the relevent mechanisms in place so that it can be removed easily and cleanly.

Also, any DLLs that are shared between applications will be handled correctly to ensure that they are not downgraded.

Dependency Walker

This utility will show you the dependencies of your application. That is, it will show you which DLLs need to be installed on a system in order for your application to function properly.

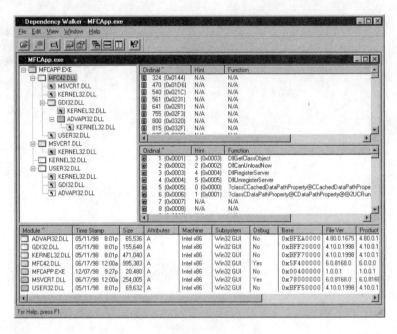

The tree view on the left hand side of the window displays the hierarchy of dependencies within your application.

As you click on the DLLs in the tree view, the other panes display information about that DLL.

The bottom pane displays information about all of the DLLs: timestamps, size, version information, etc.

The other two panes show the functions that are imported and exported by each of the DLLs. Generally this is in the form of ordinal numbers but if function names are available they will also be displayed.

Advanced Visual C++

This chapter will show you some of the more advanced features of Visual C++ such as advanced editing features and macros.

Covers

Chapter Ten

Advanced Editing

When it comes to editing your source files you have probably already noticed that Visual C++ is far from a regular text editor.

There are many advanced editing features in Visual C++. As well as the different colours that are used for keywords, there are also some advanced formatting features.

Select the 'Advanced' submenu from the 'Edit' menu.

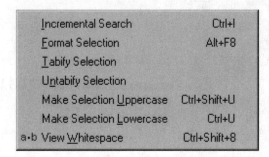

Incremental Search	Ctrl+I
Format Selection	Alt+F8
Tabify Selection	
Untabify Selection	
Make Selection Uppercase	Ctrl+Shift+U
Make Selection Lowercase	Ctrl+U
a·b View Whitespace	Ctrl+Shift+8

Those options with the word selection in them only work on the currently selected text. For example, if you want to convert a block of text to upper case, select the block of text and press 'CTRL+SHIFT+U'.

We have seen many ways of opening files into the editor: double-clicking on function in ClassView or double-clicking on files in FileView. There is another way of opening files quickly if they have been included using the #include statement.

1 Click the right mouse button on the file name in the #include statement.

2 Select the Open Document option from the menu.

Insert File into Project ▶
Open Document "MFCAppDlg.h"

Bookmarks

You may have locations in your project that you want to be able to access easily without having to search through your source files to get back to where you want to be.

Position the cursor wherever you want to add your bookmark and select 'Bookmarks' from the 'Edit' menu, or press 'ALT+F2'.

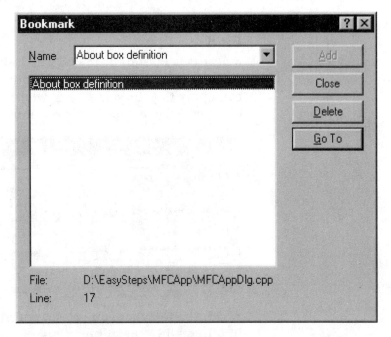

Type in a name for your bookmark and click the 'Add' button. Obviously, the Delete button deletes bookmarks from the list.

Then, in the future, when you want to go back to your bookmark you can press 'ALT+F2' to display the list of bookmarks, select one from the list and click the 'Go To' button or double-click on the bookmark that you want to go to.

Bookmarks can be browsed by using these buttons on the Edit toolbar:

Searching

The searching features of Visual C++ are very versatile indeed. There are three options on the Edit menu relating to searching: 'Find', 'Find in Files' and 'Replace'.

Find

Select this option, or press 'CTRL+F' to find a string in the current source file. There are a number of options that you can apply to your search (eg, whether to make the search case sensitive or not, the direction to search in, etc).

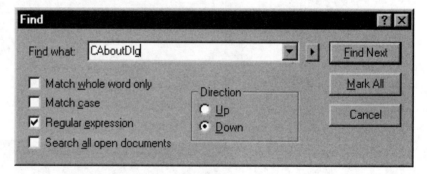

When the text that you are searching for is found, it is highlighted in the editor (as with most text editing programs) and the search will start again from that point the next time you click the 'Find Next' button.

If you click the 'Mark All' button, Visual C++ will put a mark (▢) next to every line in the file that contains the text that you are searching for.

It may be that you want to search more than one file and you don't want to perform multiple searches for some text. If you check the 'Search all open documents' checkbox, Visual C++ will search through all of the documents that are currently loaded into the editor for the string specified.

By clicking the ▶ button next to the text search field you can search for special cases such as the beginning of a line or the end of a line rather than limiting your search to text.

Find in Files

With the find in files feature of Visual C++ you are not limited to searching the files that are open in the editor. You can search any files in any folder that your computer can see. The dialog box is very similar to the Find dialog box with some key differences.

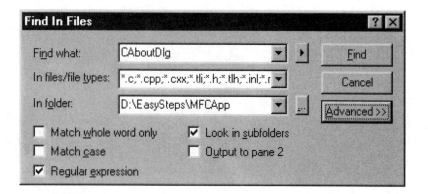

As this feature is not limited to files that are open in the editor, the text cannot be highlighted if it is found in a file that is not open. Therefore, the results are displayed in the Output window.

On the tabs at the bottom of the Output window there are two tabs for 'Find in Files'. If you check the box labelled 'Output to pane 2', the results of your search will be displayed in the second pane, otherwise they are displayed in the first pane.

You can specify the file types that Visual C++ will search and in which folder it will search for the text that you specify. Click the ▦ button to browse for a folder.

If you check the 'Look in subfolders' checkbox, Visual C++ will search in the subfolders of the folder that you specify.

As if all this wasn't advanced enough, there is an 'Advanced' button on the Find in Files dialog box which displays a list of additional folders that Visual C++ will search for the text that you have specified.

Replace

You can replace occurrences of one string with another by using the search and replace facility provided by Visual C++.

Select 'Replace' from the 'Edit' menu or press 'CTRL+H'.

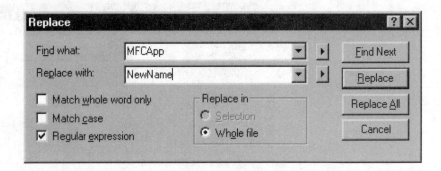

The find part of this dialog is the same as the 'Find' dialog. You can either interactively replace strings in your source files or you can ask Visual C++ to replace all occurrences of a string.

If you want Visual C++ to act on a particular block of text you can select the block in question and then set the 'Selection' radio button which will restrict Visual C++ to acting on the selected block of text.

As Visual C++ finds occurrences of your search string it will highlight the text. You can then replace this occurrence of the string by clicking the 'Replace' button. If you do not want to replace this occurrence you can click the 'Find Next' button to move on to the next occurrence.

The search and replace facility is limited to the file that is currently being edited.

Go To

If you want to jump around your source code quickly you can use the 'Go To' function of Visual C++. Select 'Go To' from the 'Edit' menu or press 'CTRL+G'.

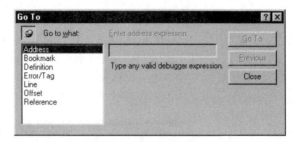

The 'Go To' dialog box will allow you to jump to different objects in your source code files including definitions of functions, bookmarks and line numbers.

As you select different items in the 'Go to what' list the text below the *address expression* field will change telling you what you need to type in the address expression field.

Note the drawing pin button in the top left corner. When the pin is in the 'Go To' dialog box ( ) it will remain displayed after you have jumped to the address specified. Otherwise, the Go To dialog box disappears as soon as you have jumped.

Inserting Files

You may have a text file or a source code file that you want to insert into the file that you are currently editing.

When you use the #include statement, you are telling the preprocessor to insert the file at that point before compiling the source code. If you want to instruct the editor to do this so that the external file becomes part of your source code you can select the 'File As Text' option from the 'Insert' menu.

You will then be prompted with the standard file browsing dialog box where you can type the name of the file that you wish to insert.

Macros

Many tasks in Visual C++ can be automated by the use of macros. The macros in Visual C++ are written using VBScript. VBScript has become very popular in the last couple of years, being used in web pages and other applications.

It is basically a cut down version of the programming language Visual Basic. There are two ways of creating macros with Visual C++: you can either edit them manually or record them.

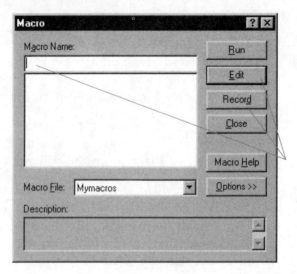

Choose macro from the 'Tools' menu and you will see the 'Macro' dialog box.

To create a new macro, type in a name and click the 'Edit' button or the 'Record' button.

Clicking the Edit button will tell Visual C++ that you want to edit the macro manually.

Either way, you will be prompted for a description for your new macro. This is optional.

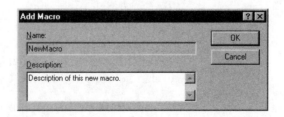

...cont'd

If you click the Record button, Visual C++ will display the Record toolbar and start recording your actions. When you click the stop button on the toolbar, Visual C++ will stop recording your macro and the macro file will then be loaded into the editor.

HANDY TIP

Macros are great for performing repetitive tasks.

You will be shown the VB subroutine that corresponds with your macro and in the body of the subroutine will be all of the actions that were recorded during the recording of your macro.

You can then edit the macro further, changing any of the existing functionality or providing new functionality. As well as all of the facilities available in VBScript, there are also many objects that are provided by Visual C++ that are specific to the development environment.

VBScript is obviously far too complicated a subject to go into here but there is a very good VBScript reference in the online help with Visual C++.

To run your macros in the future, select 'Macro' from the 'Tools' menu. You will see the Macro dialog box which now contains a list of your macros. To run a macro, simply double-click on it or select it and click the Run button.

Visual C++ also offers you the facility of creating a quick macro. This is a lot quicker and easier than creating a macro. Select 'Record Quick Macro' from the 'Tools' menu or press 'CTRL+SHIFT+R' to record the quick macro. This will behave in exactly the same way as recording a regular macro except that you will not be able to edit it afterwards. To play the macro back, select 'Play Quick Macro' from the 'Tools' menu or press 'CTRL+SHIFT+P'.

To provide easier access to your macros you can create a new toolbar or add icons to existing toolbars using the customisation features of Visual C++.

Customising Visual C++

It was mentioned in chapter one that there are many ways to customise Visual C++ and they are all accessed through the 'Customize' option on the 'Tools' menu.

There are five tabs on the 'Customize' dialog, each responsible for customising various parts of the Visual C++ environment.

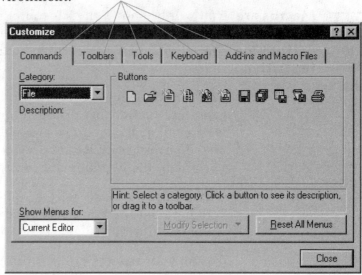

You can add your macros to toolbars by selecting the Macros category and selecting your macro.

Commands

With the commands tab you can configure the menus and toolbars for Visual C++. There are many categories of

commands for you to choose from and as you choose a category the buttons in that category will be displayed in the Buttons control.

As you click on the buttons a description of the button's action is displayed. To add the commands to a menu or a toolbar simply drag the button from the Customize dialog into the relevant place.

While the Customize dialog is being displayed, you can also drag and drop items between menus and toolbars.

Toolbars

With the toolbars tab you can customise the toolbars in Visual C++. Choose which toolbars to display by checking the relevant boxes in the list box and decide what other settings you want to apply to the toolbars by checking or clearing the boxes next to the list.

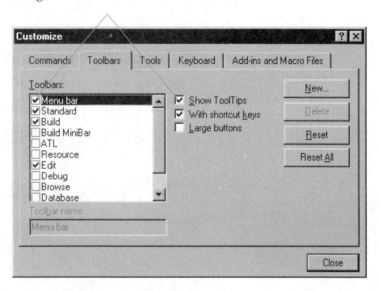

You can add a new toolbar to Visual C++ by clicking the New button.

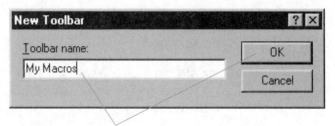

Simply enter the name of your new toolbar and click OK. An empty toolbar will now be displayed and you can configure it from the Commands tab by dragging commands onto it to create your own customised toolbar.

You can also reset individual toolbars or all of the toolbars by clicking the relevant reset button.

Tools

We have already looked at the tools customisation in the previous chapter.

Keyboard

In the keyboard tab you can customise the keyboard shortcuts that you can use in Visual C++ to trigger menu actions.

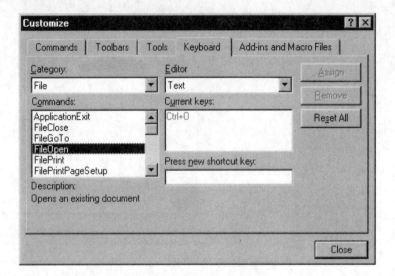

Choose a category from the list and the commands in that category will be displayed. Select a category and press a new shortcut key. When you click the Assign button the hotkey that you have pressed will be associated with the command.

Add-ins and Macro Files

Choose which add-ins and macro files you want to be loaded when Visual C++ initialises.

This option is only relevant if you have created your own Visual C++ add-in or your own macros.

When you create macros, your macro file is added automatically to the list.

Help!

This chapter will show you how to use the online help for Visual C++ and will also direct you to some good places to go for further help.

Covers

Chapter Eleven

Getting Help in Visual C++

When you install Visual C++ you should be prompted to install the online documentation and help files. This is a very good idea if you are starting with Visual C++. Also, the more that you can install to your hard disk the better, otherwise you will be swapping CDs the whole time.

The documentation that comes with Visual C++ is a cut-down version of the MSDN library. If you are not already an MSDN member then you should seriously consider it: it's not just for developers either.

As well as information on *all* of the Microsoft development products, it also contains the Microsoft knowledge bases (on all products), books, periodicals, conference papers, etc. It really is a wealth of information.

The MSDN library uses the new HTML help system so it is no longer integrated into Visual C++. To access the help system from within Visual C++ you can use any of the top three items on the 'Help' menu.

Contents
Loads the contents view of the online help. The contents are structured hierarchically in a tree view. This is useful for generally browsing the online help.

Search
You can perform quite advanced search queries using the built in search engine.

Index
The index is an alphabetical list of all of the topics in the online help. If you know what you need help on then type it in here and all relevant topics will be displayed to you.

The three menu items that we have just looked at on page 178 are specifically for accessing the online help. There are also some other options on the Help menu.

Use Extension Help

This menu item is an on/off switch for using extension help. When this item is checked, the Index, Contents and Search menu items are not used to access the online help but are used to access third party help files instead.

Check this item, then select 'Contents' from the 'Help' menu for more information about extension help.

Keyboard Map

Select this option to display a popup window which gives you information about the commands within Visual C++.

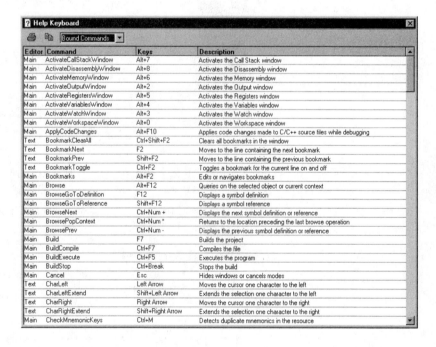

You can select which command category to display by selecting a category from the drop-down list. The default is 'Bound Commands' which shows you all of the commands in Visual C++ which are bound to a keyboard shortcut.

You can then copy this information to the keyboard or you can print it out.

Tip of the Day

Displays the tip of the day dialog box which gives you useful tips about Visual C++. While you are getting used to Visual C++ it is recommended to keep this feature active.

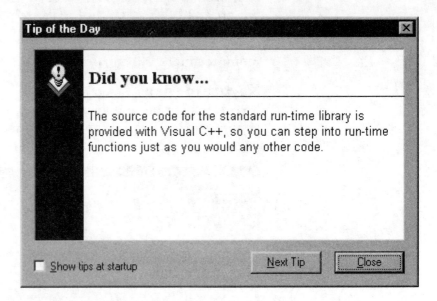

If you want to browse through the tips, you can keep clicking the 'Next Tip' button to view the tips. If you want the tips to appear every time you start Visual C++ check the 'Show tips at startup' checkbox.

Technical Support

This will take you to a page in the online help which gives you more information about getting technical support from Microsoft.

This page includes some web site addresses as well as telephone numbers, fax numbers and other information about getting technical support.

Microsoft on the Web

This submenu contains icons which are links to web pages on Microsoft's web site. When you click on them, your web browser will be launched to display them. Obviously, you will need a connection to the Internet in order to view them.

About Visual C++

If you contact Microsoft for technical support over the telephone, you will be required to give them your product ID. This is contained in the About dialog box for Visual C++:

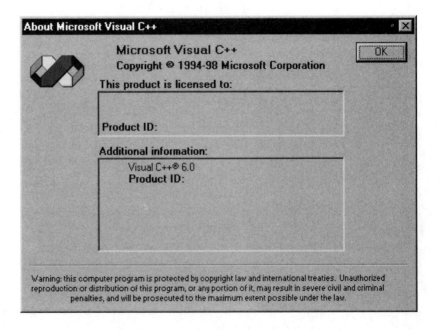

When you purchase a copy of Visual C++ you get two free technical support incidents which can be used at any time.

Technical support incidents in the UK are currently charged at £125 pounds so it is worth making your free ones count!

Using the MSDN Library

The MSDN library uses the HTML help system as a foundation but there are some added features in the library.

Active Subset   Toolbar

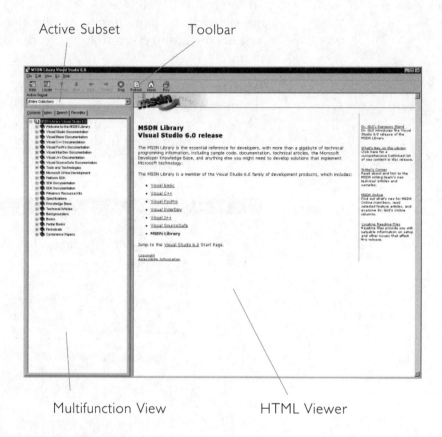

Multifunction View   HTML Viewer

Active subset

When you ask the MSDN library to perform a search, it will search the active subset for the expression that you have entered.

The default subset is the entire collection of the MSDN library, which is vast. Depending on the accuracy of your search criteria, you may end up with hundreds of documents that are completely irrelevant to what you are searching for.

...cont'd

In order to narrow down your searches, there are several subsets of information that are defined for you and you can also define your own. For example, you may only want to search the documentation for a particular SDK.

To define your own subset:

| Select 'Define Subset...' from the 'View' menu.

It's a good idea to create subsets for your most frequently used areas of MSDN.

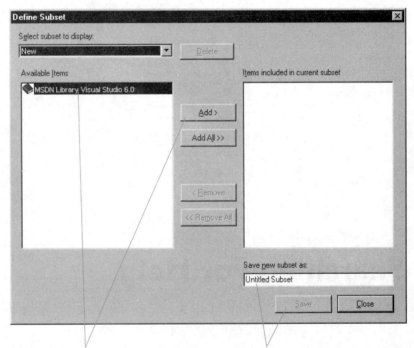

2 Define which topics you want to include in your new subset by navigating through the 'Available Items' tree. Click the Add button to add the currently selected topic to your new subset.

3 Enter a name for your new subset and click the Save button.

...cont'd

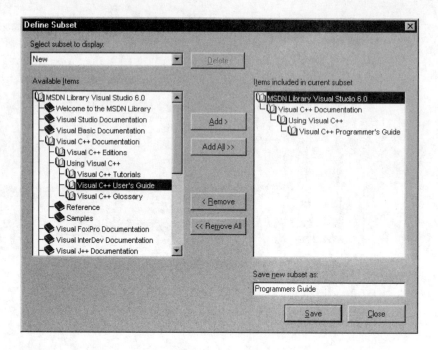

Your new subset will now be available in the list. While your subset is selected, the multifunction view will be restricted to that subset only.

Searching For Help

The MSDN library provides you with a very powerful search engine.

You can either search for a simple text string or you can perform more advanced queries.

Each word that you type into the query is treated as a separate word to search for. For example, if you typed 'MFC ClassWizard' the search engine would search for all documents containing the word 'MFC' and all documents containing the 'ClassWizard'.

...cont'd

However, if you are looking for topics relating to the MFC ClassWizard specifically, you can enclose the phrase in quotes (") and the search engine will then look for documents containing that phrase rather than documents containing each individual word. This should narrow down the response for you.

There are also some more advanced features available. If you click the ▶ button you will see that you can assign logical operators to your search criteria.

These operators help you to narrow down your search criteria if too many documents are found with your original criteria.

You can exclude words using the NOT operator or, if you are not entirely sure what you are searching for, you can use the NEAR operator which will look for words that almost match your search criteria.

There are also three checkboxes at the bottom of the results list that enable you to modify your search even further.

Search previous results

Instead of searching your whole subset again, you can narrow down your search by searching the results of your previous search.

Match similar words

Setting this option will tell the MSDN search function to match any words similar to those that you have typed in. This is the same as having the NEAR operator in front of every single word in your query.

Search titles only

Instead of searching the entire contents of every document in the library, you can ask MSDN to only search the titles of documents. This will make searches a lot quicker, but not as accurate.

Double-click on a document in the search results box to view it in the HTML view.

Generally, topics are grouped together in the library to make it easier for you to find information. If you are viewing a topic and you want to look at related topics, click on the Locate button.

 This will locate the current topic in the contents view and show you it so that you can then browse that particular area of contents to see any related topics.

Useful References

Programming is a vast topic, and there are many different aspects to it. There are many things that you may want to explore that we haven't touched on in this book, like database programming and internet programming.

However, the programming community is also vast and there are a lot of people in the world with a lot of programming knowledge.

There are web sites and newsgroups dedicated to various aspects of programming and people are generally willing to help, as long as you ask the right questions in the right places.

Newsgroups

There are many programming newsgroups. If you are having any problems and you need help, it is worth browsing through the newsgroups to see if other people are having the same problems.

If not, post an article stating your problem giving as much information as possible and someone is likely to respond.

Here are some useful programming newsgroups:

microsoft.public.win32.programmer.*

microsoft.public.vc.*

comp.os.ms-windows.programmer.*

 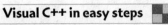

comp.programming

comp.lang.c

comp.lang.c++

The groups above that are suffixed with an asterisk (*) have groups below them. For example, *microsoft.public.win32.programmer* has different newsgroups below it relating to more specific topics like user interface programming, network programming, etc.

Web sites

As well as the menu items in the Help menu there are many other web sites related to programming that are developed by other companies or just enthusiasts.

Some sites contain frequently asked questions (FAQs): documents which have lists of questions that get asked most frequently by beginner developers along with an answer that should solve your problem.

Microsoft also have many sites relating to their various SDKs and publications, etc. Here are a few:

http://www.microsoft.com

http://www.microsoft.com/visualc

http://www.microsoft.com/mind

http://www.microsoft.com/msj

http://msdn.microsoft.com

Here are some other sites:

http://www.ddj.com

http://www.codeguru.com

http://www.dnjonline.com

http://www.progsource.com

http://www.vcdj.com

These sites are always changing, especially those that publish periodicals. It is worth visiting them regularly to get up to date information.

Most sites usually have links to download example source code too so that you can see how it's written and use it in your own programs.

Books

There are many books by many publishers about many different topics. Some books are on general programming and some are very specific to a particular area of programming such as OLE.

Code samples

Visual C++ comes with a whole host of sample applications which demonstrate various methods of programming and how things work.

The sample applications are categorised for you so that you can easily find a sample relating to the topic that you are dealing with.

Index